English Fast Lane

異文化理解のための総合英語

Tsuyoshi Kanamori
Jay Ercanbrack
Patricia Lyons
Annie Marlow
Ron Murphy
Sunao Orimoto

Cover pictures by

Photos.com

Photographs by

Ando Kimio

Arata Kikkawa

Annie Marlow

Acknowledgment

Articles on pages 23, 49-51, 57-58, 63-64, 70-71, 77-78 and 84-85 were
originally published in a slightly different form in *English Zone*,
a publication of Chukei Publishing Company,
Publishing Division of English Zone,
reprinted by permission of the authors and the publisher.

Chukei Publishing Company
Sogo Kojimachi Daiichi Bldg., 3-2 Kojimachi, Chiyoda-ku, Tokyo 102-0083

English Fast Lane

Copyright©2006 by Tsuyoshi Kanamori,
Jay Ercanbrack, Patricia Lyons, Annie Marlow, Ron Murphy, Sunao Orimoto

All rights reserved for Japan.
No part of this book may be reproduced in any form
without permission from Seibido Co., Ltd.

To Students and Teachers

The expansion of the global economy and the development of information technology are making the world seem ever smaller and more immediate. In addition, the English language is no longer the possession of its native speakers, and is becoming an effective means of communication for those who use it as a second or foreign language. English is sure to play an ever greater role in the future as an auxiliary language used not only by native speakers but also by people throughout the world for exchanging information and building relations.

Given this situation, young people need to acquire basic English ability and an understanding of language-learning methods before they become full-fledged members of society. The acquisition of specialized knowledge and accumulated experience are necessary preparation for active participation in society, of course, but the importance of improved English ability cannot be overlooked.

This textbook has been designed to allow students to acquire strategies and ways of learning English through the activation of schemata. It is also a central objective of this textbook to promote the development of the students' whole personality and sense of identity in response to the enriching experience of otherness in the text. We hope that they will enjoy learning while expanding their knowledge of various topics.

■ Textbook Organization and Use

The textbook contains 14 units. Each unit is composed of three sections: Listening Practice, Reading and Writing Practice, and Preparation for the TOEIC® Test. Activities containing vocabulary and sentence structures that will activate schemata, and listening and reading activities that expand upon them are provided. Some activities of the book can be used as classroom activities and other parts as a supplementary text for self-directed study.

In the Listening Practice activities section students become familiar with methods for learning English as a spoken language through completing tasks provided.

The reading activities, which address a wide variety of topics, ask the students to read for comprehension, but they should also be encouraged to develop and express opinions about the content later in the Speaking/Writing activities. The Summarizing and Speaking/Writing sections can be assigned as homework, either checking the answers or having students give short speeches at the beginning of the next class.

The Preparation for the TOEIC® Test section can be used at the beginning or end of each class, or the sections from several units can be combined and done at the same time.

■ Features and Use of the CD

The conversation and reading sections are recorded on the CD. The conversation is read at normal speed, with background music and sound effects to give students training in listening for comprehension in the midst of background noise.

Tsuyoshi Kanamori
on behalf of the textbook creators

はじめに
―学習者・指導者の皆様へ―

　グローバル経済圏の拡大とITの発達は世界をますます狭くし、一方で身近なものにしています。また、英語は今や母語話者の手から離れ、第二言語として使用する人々、外国語として学ぶ人たちにとっての、有効なコミュニケーションの手段となってきています。英語を母語とする人たちとのコミュニケーションの手段としてだけではなく、世界中の人々との情報交換・交流において用いられる補助的な言語として、英語の役割は更に大きくなるはずです。

　このような状況において、社会に出る前に基本的な英語力、また外国語を学ぶ方法を身につけていることはたいへん重要です。専門的な知識の獲得や経験を積み重ねながら、更に英語力を開発させていくことで、実社会で活躍する人材となることが期待できます。

　本書では、スキーマを活性化しながらの学習方略、音声言語としての英語の学び方について、そのコツを教材に取り組みながら身につけることができるように工夫をしています。また、テキストで取り上げたテーマに自分とは違う考えや存在を知ることを通して、学習者の全人的な育成をも目指しています。いろいろなトピックに関する知識も広げ、楽しみながら学んでください。

■本書の利用方法

　全部で14のユニットがあります。各ユニットは、Listening Practice, Reading and Writing Practice, Preparation for the TOEIC® Testの3つで構成され、スキーマを活性化させる語彙や構文のヒントを兼ねた練習問題、それらを利用したListening, Reading , Writing活動が準備されています。教室で行う活動として、また、一部は家庭での自主学習教材用としての補助教材としても使用することが可能です。

　Listening Practiceの活動では与えられたタスクに取り組みながら音声言語としての英語学習方法に慣れ親しんでください。

　多様なトピックを扱ったReading and Writing Practiceでは内容に対して、自分の意見を持ちながら読むだけではなく、次のSpeaking & Writing段階で自分の考えを表現することを意識しながら進めてください。Summarizing, Speaking/Writingのセクションは宿題として次回の授業の最初に答えあわせをしたり、スピーチの機会をもつなどの形で取り組むこともできます。

　Preparation for the TOEIC® Testの部分については、毎回授業の初めか最後に利用する方法もありますし、何回分かをまとめて実施することも可能です。

■準拠CDの特徴・利用法

　準拠CDには対話の部分とReading部分が収録されています。ノーマルスピードで読まれています。BGMとSE（効果音）もつけました。ノイズのある中での聞き取りの練習に取り組んでください。

執筆代表者　　金森　強

CONTENTS

Unit 1   Money! Money! Money!... 1

Unit 2   Let's Eat!... 7

Unit 3   Serving the Community... 13

Unit 4   Talking about Japan.. 20

Unit 5   Human Cloning: Do We Need It?... 27

Unit 6   Your Culture or Mine?... 33

Unit 7   City Food from Field to Table... 40

Unit 8   The Making of a Nobel Prize-winner.................................... 47

Unit 9   Walking for Health: Yours and the Earth's........................... 54

Unit 10 Changing Lives... 61

Unit 11 How Fast Can We Travel?.. 68

Unit 12 Medical Care for the Whole Person..................................... 75

Unit 13 Looking for a Job?.. 82

Unit 14 Follow Your Dreams... 89

Money! Money! Money!

LISTENING PRACTICE

Warm-up Activity I: Vocabulary and Phrases

What qualities or things do you consider most important for a boyfriend or girlfriend to have? Rank your top five choices and choose the correct meaning for the following words or phrases (1) to (16).

(Rank / meaning)
(/) good looks   (/) good personality   (/) sense of humor
(/) kindness   (/) honesty   (/) similar interests
(/) a car   (/) good cook   (/) faithfulness
(/) similar values   (/) intelligence   (/) money
(/) generosity   (/) patience   (/) good job
(/) good voice

(1) ability to appreciate the funny or amusing ユーモア感覚　　(2) automobile 車
(3) enjoyment of the same things 共通の興味　　(4) what we use to buy things お金
(5) pleasant vocal sounds きれいな声　　(6) always telling the truth 正直さ
(7) giving freely and willingly 寛大さ　　(8) attractive and interesting qualities of character 性格のよさ　　(9) ability to think, understand, and learn well 知性
(10) ability to accept difficulty or unpleasantness 我慢強さ　　(11) considering the same things to be important 共通の価値観　　(12) physical attractiveness 容姿のよさ
(13) gentleness and caring for others やさしさ　　(14) ability to prepare delicious dishes 料理の腕　　(15) work that pays well or has a good future いい仕事　　(16) being true to one's partner 浮気をしないこと

B. Warm-up Activity II

If you agree with the following ideas, write A (=agree). If you don't, write D (=disagree).

1. Money is the most important point to consider when choosing a marriage partner.
 ( )
2. Money should not be considered when choosing a marriage partner. ( )
3. Even if two people love each other, they cannot be happy without money. ( )
4. Money can't buy happiness. ( )
5. If two people love and respect each other, they can lead a happy life together. ( )

C. Listening Practice

Listen to the conversation and fill in the blanks. Then practice reading with a partner.

Amy: When I first saw Japanese money, I thought it looked like money from "Monopoly." Maybe because it was very _____.

Masaharu: When I first saw a dollar _____, I thought it looked like play money too. Maybe all foreign money seems like that.

Amy: What's worse is how a little piece of paper can mean so much. It causes _____, _____ _____, and even war!

Masaharu: It really does mean a lot. Money can _____ the world. Back to the _____ of bills… did you know that there is a special picture on a Japanese bill that you can only see when you hold it up to the light?

Amy: Oh, yes. That's called a watermark. There's one on American bills too.

Masaharu: Well, I'll bet* you can't tell me whose _____ is on a thousand yen bill.

Amy: And I'll bet you can't tell me whose picture is on a one dollar bill.

Masaharu: Uhhh… Abraham Lincoln?

Amy: Shōtoku Taishi?

*I'll bet…. = I'm almost certain that….

Listen to the CD and write the questions. Then listen to the conversation again and answer the questions.

1. _____

2. _____

3. _____

4. _____

Reading and Writing Practice

Words and Phrases

denomination 貨幣単位　　note 紙幣　　currency 通貨, 貨幣　　replace 〜に取って代わる　　appoint 任命する　　committee 委員会　　get rid of 廃止する　　sugar cane mill 製糖工場　　nervously 神経質に　　enemy 敵　　invasion 侵略　　take action 行動を起こす　　accordingly それに応じて　　distribution 分配　　territory 領土　　legal tender 法定通貨　　consist of 〜から成る　　seal 印　　serial number 通し番号　　bill 紙幣　　letter 文字　　no longer もはや〜ではない　　due to 〜のために　　resistance 抵抗　　complete 完了する　　in circulation 流通して　　roughly およそ　　dispose of 廃棄する　　attempt 試み　　enormous quantity of 莫大な量の　　remove 廃棄する　　haul 運ぶ　　smell におい

True-False Questions

Read the questions below, and then read the following passage to find the answers.

1. In January 1942, special notes were imprinted with the word "Hawai'i".　　T / F
2. The new money was used even outside Hawai'i and throughout North America.　　T / F
3. There were four denominations in Hawai'i.　　T / F
4. The new notes were green and blue, like U.S. currency.　　T / F
5. The old money was replaced by the new within a year without any resistance.　　T / F
6. The government appointed a special committee to get rid of $200 million.　　T / F
7. The old money was collected and burned at a sugar cane mill.　　T / F

Let's Read!

"New Money" for Hawai'i

　In January 1942, one month after Pearl Harbor was attacked, the U.S. government nervously feared an enemy invasion. It decided to take action accordingly. One of the first steps taken was to create "New Money." Planned for distribution in the summer of '42, special notes imprinted with the word "Hawai'i" would become legal tender in the territory but would have no value outside of Hawai'i itself. This money was to consist of $1, $5, $10 and $20 denominations. Brown seals and serial numbers would replace the green and blue ones normally found on U.S. currency. The word "Hawai'i" would appear twice on the front of each bill and once in large letters across the back. The old money would no longer be legal tender in Hawai'i, and so would be collected and destroyed. However, due to citizen resistance, it took 27 months to complete the change and to have the new money out in circulation. The government then put together a special committee to get rid of roughly 200 million dollars of old money. It was difficult to find a way to dispose of the enormous quantity of notes. After a few failed attempts to remove it, the money was finally hauled to a sugar cane mill on O'ahu and burned. Two hundred million dollars went up in smoke...but they say it had a very sweet smell!   (227 words)

◆D◆ Summarizing

Read the paragraph again and write appropriate words or phrases in the spaces.

In January 1942, one month after Pearl Harbor was attacked, the U.S. government nervously feared a Japanese _____. It decided to take action accordingly. One of the first steps taken was to create "New Money." Planned for distribution in the _____ of '42, special notes would be imprinted with the word "Hawai'i" and would become legal tender in the _____, but they would not be used _____ _____ Hawai'i.

This money _____ _____ $1, $5, $10 and $20 denominations. While green seals and blue numbers were normally found on _____ _____, the new money's seals and numbers were _____. The word _____ would appear _____ _____ on the bill. The old money was _____ and _____ because it would no longer be legal tender in Hawai'i anymore.

It took 27 months to complete the change and to have the new money out in circulation because of _____ _____. The government then put together a _____ _____ to get rid of roughly 200 million dollars of old money. It was not _____ to find a way to dispose of the enormous _____ of notes.

Although some attempts to remove it _____, the money was carried to a sugar cane mill on O'ahu and _____. Two hundred million dollars went up in smoke... but _____ _____ that it had a very sweet smell!

◆E◆ Speaking/Writing

1. Talk about your first impression of "foreign" money and tell a non-Japanese friend about Japanese bills.

2. If you could change the pictures of people on Japanese money, whose pictures would you choose? Why?

Preparation for the TOEIC® TEST

Unit 1

Part 1 — Photographs

Look at each picture and listen to four statements. Choose the statement that best describes each picture.

1.
Ⓐ Ⓑ Ⓒ Ⓓ

2.
Ⓐ Ⓑ Ⓒ Ⓓ

Part 2 — Question-Response

Listen to a question followed by three responses and then choose the best response.

3. Mark your answer on your answer sheet.   Ⓐ Ⓑ Ⓒ
4. Mark your answer on your answer sheet.   Ⓐ Ⓑ Ⓒ
5. Mark your answer on your answer sheet.   Ⓐ Ⓑ Ⓒ
6. Mark your answer on your answer sheet.   Ⓐ Ⓑ Ⓒ

Part 3 — Short Conversation

Listen to a short conversation and answer the three questions below.

7. Where are the speakers?   Ⓐ Ⓑ Ⓒ Ⓓ
   (A) Outside the library
   (B) Sitting at a library table
   (C) At the librarian's desk
   (D) Next to a library bookshelf

8. What is the woman's problem?
   (A) The library has already closed.
   (B) She cannot find an important book.
   (C) She has forgotten to bring back a book.
   (D) The library does not stock the book she wants.

9. Who does the man suggest might have the book?
   (A) Another person in the library
   (B) The librarian
   (C) One of the woman's fellow students
   (D) The woman's professor

Part 4 — Short Talk

Listen to a short talk and answer the three questions below.

10. Which one of the following beliefs is the argument of the lecture?
    (A) In the future, English will be the only world language spoken by everyone for business and daily life.
    (B) In the future, being bilingual or multilingual will be an advantage.
    (C) In the future, monolingual English speakers will have an advantage.
    (D) In the future, most people will be able to speak only one language.

11. What are the major languages?
    (A) English, Mandarin, Latin, Hindi and Spanish.
    (B) English, Mandarin, Portuguese, Arabic and Spanish.
    (C) English, Mandarin, Spanish, Hindi and Arabic.
    (D) English, Mandarin, Spanish, French and Arabic.

12. According to the lecture, what kind of people will businesses need?
    (A) Multilingual people.
    (B) People with excellent English communication skills.
    (C) Multi-skilled people.
    (D) People with an interest in all cultures.

Let's Eat!

LISTENING PRACTICE

A. Warm-up Activity I: Vocabulary and Phrases

Choose the correct meaning for the following words or phrases from (1) to (14).

(　　) cuisine　　　　(　　) specialty　　　　(　　) custom
(　　) diet　　　　　(　　) can't wait to　　　(　　) stay up (late)
(　　) kind of like the ones on TV　　　　　 (　　) be supposed to
(　　) pick up　　　 (　　) bowl　　　　　　(　　) plate
(　　) slurp　　　　 (　　) embarrassing　　　(　　) silly

(1) a style of cooking 料理：フランス料理，中華料理など　　(2) to be expected to do something ～することになっている　　(3) causing someone to look or feel awkward or stupid 恥ずかしい　　(4) an accepted way of doing things in society 慣習　　(5) a deep round container for holding food お椀　　(6) to want to do something as soon as possible 早く～したい　　(7) to lift 持ち上げる　　(8) similar to what one might see on television テレビで見るような　　(9) the foods that you usually eat / foods that you eat in order to lose weight 普通の食事，ダイエット食　　(10) to make a loud noise while drinking something 音を立てて飲む　　(11) a flat, usually round, dish for food 皿　　(12) to not go to bed until a late hour 遅くまで起きている　　(13) something that someone is good at 得意なもの　　(14) foolish, ridiculous 思慮がない，愚かな

B. Warm-up Activity II

1. Which cuisine(s) do you like?
2. Do you enjoy cooking? If so, what's your specialty?
3. Do you know some eating customs of other countries that are different from Japan's?
4. Do you think you have a well-balanced diet?
5. Do you usually eat faster (or slower) than other people?

Listening Practice

Listen to the conversation and fill in the blanks. Then practice reading with a partner.

At a potluck party

Max: Yasu, welcome back. How _____ your trip?

Yasu: Well, it wasn't my first time abroad, but even so, I _____ a lot of new things. I stayed with a family in the United States, and I really experienced… uhh… what do you call it… culture shock.

Max: I can't wait to hear about it, but first, let's eat. You have to try my *chirashizushi*. I stayed up all night trying to get it right. What did you bring?

Yasu: I brought dogs.

Max: Dogs….? I'm afraid we won't have enough food for pets, too.

Yasu: Oh, they're not animals. You know, they're kind of like sausage but made from different meats _____ together, and they're eaten between _____ of bread.

Max: Oh, hotdogs! Let me try one. Mmm, not bad. So tell me about your home-stay family.

Yasu: Well, they're really nice, kind of like the families you see on TV. They have two kids and a dog. But I _____ had trouble at dinnertime.

Max: What do you mean?

Yasu: You know how in Japan we're supposed to pick up our rice bowl when we eat? Well, I got _____ looks when I picked up my plate and started eating, and when I slurped my soup, the kids started to laugh.

Max: I told you about slurping your soup. Did you forget? And I told you to eat soup with a spoon.

Yasu: I guess you did. Even going out to eat was embarrassing. Did you know that everybody orders their own food, _____ of just one person talking to the waiter? I thought my home-stay family was going to order for me but everybody just waited for me to _____ it myself.

Max: You must _____ looked very silly.

Listen to the CD and write the questions. Then listen to the conversation again and answer the questions.

1. _____

_____

2. _____

_____

3. _____
_____

4. _____
_____

Reading and Writing Practice

Words and Phrases

better 〈記録を〉更新する   gluttony 大食   feature 特集する   exhibit 示す
be associated with ～と結びつく   annual 年一度の   competition 競争   dominate 制覇する   previous 以前の   pounder 体重が～ポンドのある人   earn 〈名声や評判を〉得る   achieve 手に入れる，成し遂げる   celebrity 有名人   status 地位   via ～を媒介として   assumed the trappings of a sport 華やかなスポーツとみなされるようになった   refine 〈技を〉みがく   stretch 大きくする   stomach 胃   abruptly 急に   choke 窒息する   subsequently その後   venue 開催場

B True-False Questions

Read the questions below, and then read the following passage to find the answers.

1. Hotdogs are a popular food in America.　　　　　　　　　　　　T / F
2. A hotdog eating contest is held every year on the 4th of July.　　T / F
3. Since 1916 the champion of the contest each year has been an American.　T / F
4. Takeru Kobayashi has bettered the record every contest.　　　　T / F
5. Kobayashi is a big wrestler nicknamed "The Prince."　　　　　　T / F
6. Gluttony contests are considered to be a sport, and many TV programs in Japan have featured them.　　　　　　　　　　　　　　　　　　　T / F
7. Kobayashi will at least have chances to exhibit his skills in the United States, if not in Japan.　　　　　　　　　　　　　　　　　　　　　T / F

C Let's Read!

Food Fighters

　　Nothing could be more American than hotdogs. To many Americans they are closely associated with 4th of July picnics and baseball games, and the annual July 4th hotdog eating contest, begun in 1916 by a famous hotdog restaurant, is an event that seems made for this nation of big eaters. Until 1996 the champion each year was an American, but since then the competition has been dominated by the Japanese.

The 2004 contest was won by Takeru "Tsunami" Kobayashi, when he bettered the record he had set in 2002, 50½ hotdogs eaten in 12 minutes, by eating 53½. The 130-pounder's rock star looks have earned him another nickname in Japan, "The Prince." He is one of a group of young "food fighters" who achieved celebrity status via dramatically staged eating contests on Japanese television. Gluttony, or *ōgui* in Japanese, may have been considered a terrible sin in the past, but recently it has assumed the trappings of a sport. By refining their techniques and stretching their stomachs, Japanese competitors have risen to the top internationally.

Programs featuring eating contests disappeared abruptly from Japanese TV screens early in 2002 after a 14-year-old junior high school student choked during a lunch time speed-eating attempt and subsequently died. Without this venue, the future of professional eaters like Kobayashi is uncertain, but they will probably have at least one place to exhibit their skills as long as Americans continue to eat hotdogs.

(238 words)

D Summarizing

Read the paragraph again and write appropriate words or phrases in the spaces.

Hotdogs are a very _____ food in North America. Many Americans associate hotdogs with _____ _____ _____ _____ and _____ _____. The champion of the contest had been _____ _____ until 1996, after which the competition was dominated by _____ _____. Takeru "Tsunami" Kobayashi won the contest in 2004, _____ _____ _____ he had set in _____. He _____ 53½ hotdogs in 12 minutes. Kobayashi is _____ _____ he is a member of a group of _____ _____ who achieved _____ _____ via Japanese TV programs. Japanese competitors have risen to the top internationally by _____ _____ _____ and _____ _____ _____.

Because a 14-year-old junior high student choked during a _____ _____ _____ and subsequently died, such TV programs _____ from Japanese TV screens. But Kobayashi will probably have _____ _____ one place to exhibit his skills _____ _____ _____ Americans continue to eat hotdogs.

E Speaking/Writing

1. What do you think about eating contests? Should they be shown on TV? Why or why not?

2. "Comfort food" is food that makes us feel good and happy when we eat it, especially when we have been feeling bad or unhappy. Often it's something our mothers prepared for us. Tell about your "comfort food."

Preparation for the TOEIC® TEST

Unit 2

Part 1 — Photographs

Look at each picture and listen to four statements. Choose the statement that best describes each picture.

1.

   Ⓐ Ⓑ Ⓒ Ⓓ

2.

   Ⓐ Ⓑ Ⓒ Ⓓ

Part 2 — Question-Response

Listen to a question followed by three responses and then choose the best response.

3. Mark your answer on your answer sheet.   Ⓐ Ⓑ Ⓒ
4. Mark your answer on your answer sheet.   Ⓐ Ⓑ Ⓒ
5. Mark your answer on your answer sheet.   Ⓐ Ⓑ Ⓒ
6. Mark your answer on your answer sheet.   Ⓐ Ⓑ Ⓒ

Part 3 — Short Conversation

Listen to a short conversation and answer the three questions below.

7. Why did the woman not buy the house?   Ⓐ Ⓑ Ⓒ Ⓓ
   (A) Her offer was too low.
   (B) She did not like it.
   (C) It was badly damaged.
   (D) It had already been sold.

Unit 2 *Let's Eat!*   11

8. What does the man want to know?
    (A) Whether the woman will increase her offer
    (B) How much she is willing to pay
    (C) Whether she has looked at other houses
    (D) Who bought the house

9. How much extra does the woman think she would have to spend?
    (A) $5,000
    (B) $15,000
    (C) $50,000
    (D) $500,000

Part 4 — Short Talk

Listen to a short talk and answer the three questions below.

10. Where are the passengers?
    (A) On a bus.
    (B) On a plane.
    (C) On a ferry.
    (D) On a cruise ship.

11. What is about to happen?
    (A) They are about to land.
    (B) There is a storm ahead.
    (C) A meal is about to be served.
    (D) The seatbelt sign will be turned off.

12. Who made the announcement?
    (A) The pilot.
    (B) The co-pilot.
    (C) A cabin attendant.
    (D) The tour leader.

Serving the Community

LISTENING PRACTICE

A. Warm-up Activity I: Vocabulary and Phrases

Choose the correct meaning for the following words or phrases from (1) to (13).

( ) community service ( ) credit ( ) evaluate
( ) requirement ( ) orphanage ( ) piggyback ride
( ) sensitive ( ) be sure to ( ) definitely
( ) hurt ( ) tiring ( ) get the hang of
( ) rewarding

(1)giving the feeling that it's worth doing やりがいのある   (2)to learn how to do something こつをつかむ, 慣れる   (3)to cause pain 傷つける   (4)a unit of study 単位   (5)certainly 絶対に   (6)an institution where children without parents live 孤児院   (7)to form an opinion about the value or quality of something 評価する   (8)becoming hurt or unhappy easily 敏感な   (9)making you feel the need to rest つかれさせる, きつい   (10)local volunteer work 地域奉仕   (11)a course necessary for advancement or graduation 必修科目   (12)carrying someone on one's back おんぶ   (13)to do without fail 必ず〜する

B. Warm-up Activity II

If you agree with the following ideas, write A (=agree). If you don't, write D (=disagree).

1. Students should be required to do community service. ( )
2. It's a good idea for schools to give credit to students who do community service. ( )
3. Schools should make clear how they will evaluate students doing community service. ( )

13

4. It's good for students to learn skills through real-life activities, rather than through books.   ( )
5. Professors also should volunteer for community service.   ( )

◆C◆ Listening Practice

Listen to the conversation and fill in the blanks. Then practice reading with a partner. ₈ CD

Bonnie: Eriko, I _____ you're going to start doing some community service next Monday.
Eriko: Yes, it's a requirement for my _____ in college.
Bonnie: What are you going to be doing?
Eriko: I'll be doing _____ work at an orphanage.
Bonnie: Actually, I did that _____ myself. Would you like a little advice?
Eriko: Of course.
Bonnie: Do not, I _____, do not give any piggyback rides, or you'll be giving them _____ day. If you give a piggyback ride to one kid, all the others will come and ask for one. At the end of the day you'll have a "piggybackache". If I hadn't given any, I would have _____ a lot better.
Eriko: Thanks. I'll remember that.
Bonnie: And don't forget that the kids may be _____ very sensitive about not having a family or really interested in what it's like to have one. So you'll have to be extra careful when talking with them.
Eriko: I'll be sure to remember that. I don't want to _____ anyone's feelings.
Bonnie: Of course not. So, good luck. The work is very _____ at first, but once you get the hang of it, it's really fun and _____.

Listen to the CD and write the questions. Then listen to the conversation again and answer the questions. ₉ CD

1. _____
   _____
2. _____
   _____
3. _____
   _____
4. _____
   _____

Reading and Writing Practice

Words and Phrases

graduate from ～を卒業する　　provide 提供する　　significant 意味のある　　mandatory 強制の　　require 要求する　　local その地域の　　valuable 価値のある　　description 説明　　role 役割　　improve 改善する　　participant 参加者　　be encouraged to ～するよう勧められる　　contribution 貢献　　participate in ～に参加する　　fix up 修理する　　elementary school 小学校　　four-hour shift 4時間交代制　　a minimum of 最低でも～　　challenged 障害のある　　emotionally 情緒的に　　physically 肉体的に　　inner-city 都心部の　　senior citizens homes 養老院　　childcare facilities 保育施設　　complete やり遂げる　　at-risk youth 非行に走る可能性のある若者　　renovation 改善　　reservation 保留地　　obtain 手に入れる

True-False Questions

Read the questions below, and then read the following passage to find the answers.

1. Some students in the U.S. have to do community service to graduate from school.　　T / F
2. The schools believe community service provides their students significant experiences.　　T / F
3. Students must make action plans for changing their parents.　　T / F
4. Students work with a family member on a community project.　　T / F
5. Each student has to work more than 12 hours a day with his/her parents.　　T / F
6. Students have to do something that people think is impossible within 50 hours.　　T / F
7. After doing community service, students have to write essays and make presentations about their experience.　　T / F

Let's Read!

Should community service for students be mandatory?

Some high schools in the U.S. require their students to do community service (local volunteer work) in order to graduate. These schools believe that such service provides a valuable education that cannot be achieved through books. Here is a description of the community service program at Jesuit High School in Sacramento, California.

Family

Students are expected to write about their roles within their family. Then they must create an "action plan" by which they can improve their relationships with other family members. Finally, students spend five hours on a community service project with at least one other family member as an active participant.

Community

Students, as a group, are encouraged to make a significant contribution to the local community. All students, and many of their parents, participate in fixing up a local elementary school. Each student is required to work one four-hour shift.

Students as agents of social change

Students are required to work a minimum of 50 hours in the community with persons who are in some way "challenged," either mentally, emotionally, physically, academically or economically. Students often choose to volunteer at inner-city schools, senior citizens homes, childcare facilities, or hospitals which help "challenged" patients. Students can complete their service projects during the summer. Summer programs include camps for "challenged" children and adults, day camps for at-risk youth, renovation on Native American reservations, and helping the poor in Tijuana, Mexico. When finished, students must write a five-page essay and do a presentation to the class and teachers.

(254 words)

D Summarizing

Read the paragraph again and write appropriate words or phrases in the spaces.

Some high schools in the U.S. _____ their students to do community service, in other words, _____ _____ _____, in order to _____ from school. Students are believed to obtain a _____ _____ through such experience.

Students have to write about _____ _____ within the family. They are expected to _____ their relationships with _____ _____ _____ through action plans they _____. Finally, students and at least _____ _____ _____ _____ spend five hours on a community service project.

Students, as a group, are challenged to make a _____ _____ to the local community. All students, and many _____ _____ _____, _____ _____ fixing up a local elementary school. Each student must work one _____ _____.

Students are required to work for _____ _____ 50 hours in the community with people who are "challenged" _____ _____ _____, either mentally emotionally, physically, academically or economically. Students often _____ _____ _____ at inner-city schools, senior citizens homes, childcare facilities, or hospitals which serve "challenged" patients. Students can complete their service projects _____ _____ _____. After summer programs they have to _____ _____ _____ _____ and _____ _____ _____.

Speaking/Writing

1. Write your views on having community service be a requirement for your graduation.

2. Have you done community service before? What did you do? How do you feel about the experience?

Preparation for the TOEIC® TEST

Unit 3

Part 1 — Photographs

Look at each picture and listen to four statements. Choose the statement that best describes each picture.

1. Ⓐ Ⓑ Ⓒ Ⓓ

2. Ⓐ Ⓑ Ⓒ Ⓓ

Part 2 — Question-Response

Listen to a question followed by three responses and then choose the best response.

3. Mark your answer on your answer sheet.   Ⓐ Ⓑ Ⓒ
4. Mark your answer on your answer sheet.   Ⓐ Ⓑ Ⓒ
5. Mark your answer on your answer sheet.   Ⓐ Ⓑ Ⓒ
6. Mark your answer on your answer sheet.   Ⓐ Ⓑ Ⓒ

Part 3 — Short Conversation

Listen to a short conversation and answer the three questions below.

7. Why does the woman not want to climb the mountain?   Ⓐ Ⓑ Ⓒ Ⓓ
   (A) She has never climbed a mountain before.
   (B) The weather is too bad.
   (C) She is not in good physical condition.
   (D) The mountain is too high.

8. What does the man tell her? Ⓐ Ⓑ Ⓒ Ⓓ
    (A) The mountain is not very high.
    (B) The climb is easier than it appears to be.
    (C) It is too late to start now.
    (D) They should have a rest before starting.

9. What does the woman want to do before the climb? Ⓐ Ⓑ Ⓒ Ⓓ
    (A) Have breakfast
    (B) Get food and water
    (C) Put on her boots
    (D) Look at a map

Part 4 — Short Talk

Listen to a short talk and answer the three questions below.

10. What happened? Ⓐ Ⓑ Ⓒ Ⓓ
    (A) A group of elementary school students were hit by a train while crossing railway tracks near their school.
    (B) A train crashed into an elementary school.
    (C) A new high speed train derailed and crashed.
    (D) A train took the wrong turn.

11. How many people were killed? Ⓐ Ⓑ Ⓒ Ⓓ
    (A) Up to 40 people.
    (B) At least 40 people.
    (C) 30 passengers and 10 students
    (D) Some of the people in the front two carriages.

12. Why did the accident occur? Ⓐ Ⓑ Ⓒ Ⓓ
    (A) Noisy passengers caused the accident.
    (B) The railway line runs too close to the school.
    (C) It is not yet known.
    (D) The train went off the tracks.

Talking about Japan

LISTENING PRACTICE

A Warm-up Activity I: Vocabulary and Phrases

Choose the correct meaning for the following words or phrases from (1) to (17).

( ) domestic   ( ) self-sufficiency   ( ) rate
( ) common   ( ) cause   ( ) cancer
( ) cerebral stroke ( ) diabetes   ( ) invent
( ) disposable   ( ) backed up   ( ) way back in time
( ) I don't get it. ( ) found   ( ) have something to do with
( ) cell phone   ( ) average life expectancy

(1) mobile telephone 携帯電話   (2) average number of years that people live 平均寿命   (3) to start an organization or institution 創設する   (4) ability to provide one's needs by oneself 自給   (5) disease in which cells grow abnormally and kill healthy cells 癌   (6) related to things inside a country 国内の   (7) illness caused when a blood vessel in the brain bursts or is blocked 脳卒中   (8) a fixed ratio between two things 率，割合   (9) illness caused by lack of insulin 糖尿病   (10) the thing that makes something happen 原因   (11) to make something that has not existed before 発明する   (12) made to be thrown away after use 使い捨ての   (13) a long time ago はるか昔の   (14) to be related to 関係がある   (15) I don't understand. わかりません   (16) lined up behind a blockage 渋滞した   (17) happening often 一般的な

B Warm-up Activity II

Answer the following questions.

1. Who was Japan's first Nobel Prize winner?
   a. Susumu Tonegawa   b. Yasunari Kawabata
   c. Hideki Yukawa   d. Leo Esaki

2. What was Japan's domestic food self-sufficiency rate in 2002?
   a. 70%   b. 60%   c. 50%   d. 40%

3. What is the most common cause of death in Japan?
   a. heart disease   b. cancer   c. cerebral stroke   d. diabetes

4. Who invented the floppy disk?
   a. Dr. Shirakawa   b. Dr. Fukui   c. Dr. Koshiba   d. Dr. Nakamatsu

5. Which Japanese company produced the first "disposable camera"?
   a. Fuji Photo Film Co., Ltd.   b. Canon Inc.
   c. Konica Minolta Holdings, Inc.   d. Nikon

C Listening Practice

Listen to the conversation and fill in the blanks. Then practice reading with a partner.

George: During the Japanese festival, the streets are crowded and _____ is backed up a mile. Why in the world is there a Japanese Culture Day in America anyway? I mean, we never had "samurais" or "ninjas" before, and who in America likes raw _____?

Tetsuya: You know, you may be right about *samurai* and *ninja*. But what you're talking about is Japanese _____. Way back in time!

George: So?

Tetsuya: Nowadays you have a lot of Japanese things in America.

George: You _____ my Honda?

Tetsuya: Yes! You know that Honda is a Japanese name, don't you? And how about your _____?

George: Bridgestone?

Tetsuya: That company was _____ by a Japanese man named Ishibashi.

George: What does that have to do with it?

Tetsuya: In Japanese, *ishi* means stone, and *bashi* means bridge.

George: Uh-huh.

Tetsuya: Let me see your cell phone.

George: OK.

Tetsuya: Aha! Just as I _____! A Japanese-made Sony!

George: I guess we have a lot to do with Japanese culture. I need to _____ more about it. What else is there?

Tetsuya: Well, we have the _____ life expectancy...even karate is Japanese...and...

Listen to the CD and write the questions. Then listen to the conversation again and answer the questions.

1. _____
2. _____
3. _____
4. _____

READING AND WRITING PRACTICE

A Words and Phrases

capital 首都   locate 位置する   region 地域   low-fat diet 脂肪分の少ない食事   export 輸出品   dairy products 乳製品   chemicals 化学薬品   divorce 離婚   strict 厳しい   homicide 殺人   highly populated 人口の多い   climate 気候   vary 異なる   humid 湿気が多い   current 現在の   metropolitan 大都市の   tend to ～する傾向がある   longevity 長生き   vehicle 乗り物   ceramics 陶器   natural resources 天然資源   petroleum 石油   cultivate 栽培する   get married 結婚する   all-time high 空前の高さ、史上最高の   such as たとえば   capital punishment 死刑   unlike ～と違って   prisoner 囚人   execution 死刑執行

B True-False Questions

Read the questions below, and then read the following passage to find the answers.

1. Tokyo, the capital of Japan, is located in the Kansai region of the main island.   T / F
2. More than 10% of the Japanese population live in Tokyo.   T / F
3. Japan's low-fat diet is believed to be the reason for the long life expectancy.   T / F
4. Japan's major exports include dairy products, chemicals, and cameras.   T / F
5. The current divorce rate is more than 2%.   T / F
6. Gun control is strict in the US, and the homicide rate is low.   T / F
7. There is more than one religion in Japan.   T / F

Let's Read!

Talking about Japan

About geography

☆ Tokyo is not only Japan's largest and most highly populated city, it's also Japan's capital. It's located in the Kanto region of Honshu, the main island.

☆ The climate in Japan can vary from extremely cold in winter to hot and humid in summer, with a rainy season in June and July. Spring and autumn seasons are generally mild.

About population

☆ The current population of Japan is over 126 million, with about 12 million people living in the Tokyo metropolitan area. Over 3 million people live in Yokohama and over 2 million in Osaka.

☆ The average life expectancy of the Japanese is the longest in the world, with women living to an average of 85 and men of 78. People on the island of Okinawa tend to live even longer, quite a few past the age of 100. Many reports say the reason for the longevity is Japan's standard low-fat diet.

About the economy

☆ In addition to its well-known motor vehicles, Japan's major exports include electronics, telecommunications products, industrial machinery, chemicals, and ceramics.

☆ Japan is not rich in natural resources, and it must import nearly all its petroleum. Also, because it has so many mountains, and it is difficult to cultivate crops, Japan must also import more than half of its food.

About lifestyle

☆ These days, Japanese people are getting married later in life. The average marriage age is 30 for men and 28 for women.

☆ Divorce used to be taboo in Japan, but the current divorce rate is at an all-time high, with 2.3 divorces for every 1,000 people. Even Prime Minister Koizumi was divorced!

About politics

☆ Gun control is very strict in Japan, as it is in the UK, and this might be the reason why the homicide rate is much lower than in other countries, such as the U.S.

☆ Capital punishment by hanging is legal in Japan, as it is in the United States, and is supported by the majority of the public. But unlike other countries, prisoners in Japan never know the day of their execution.

About religion

☆ Shinto and Buddhism are considered to be the main religions of Japan. There is also a small percentage of Christians.   (374 words; adapted from "Magic Phrases: When Talking About Japan," *English Zone*, no. 7, January 2004.)

D. Summarizing

Read the paragraph again and write appropriate words or phrases in the spaces. From this unit you may need to write more than one word in each space.

Japan has a _____ in June and July, and it is very _____ and _____ in summer. There is usually mild weather in _____.

The average life expectancy of Japanese women is 85, while for men it's 78. In Okinawa _____ people live more than _____. The Japanese _____ diet is regarded as good for _____ and the main reason for the long _____.

Japan has to import _____ because it is not rich in natural resources. Also, it must import _____ because there are so many mountains and it is difficult to cultivate crops in Japan.

Divorce _____ regarded as bad in Japan, but the divorce _____ is higher than ever, with 2.3 divorces for every 1,000 people.

_____ other countries, prisoners _____ in Japan never know when they will be _____.

The main _____ of Japan are Shinto and Buddhism. The percentage of Christians is _____.

E. Speaking/Writing

1. What are some other interesting facts about Japan that people from other countries should know?

2. Which Japanese person would you like to introduce to the world?

Preparation for the TOEIC® TEST

Unit 4

Part 1 — Photographs

14 CD

Look at each picture and listen to four statements. Choose the statement that best describes each picture.

1. Ⓐ Ⓑ Ⓒ Ⓓ

2. Ⓐ Ⓑ Ⓒ Ⓓ

Part 2 — Question-Response

15 CD

Listen to a question followed by three responses and then choose the best response.

3. Mark your answer on your answer sheet. Ⓐ Ⓑ Ⓒ
4. Mark your answer on your answer sheet. Ⓐ Ⓑ Ⓒ
5. Mark your answer on your answer sheet. Ⓐ Ⓑ Ⓒ
6. Mark your answer on your answer sheet. Ⓐ Ⓑ Ⓒ

Part 3 — Short Conversation

16 CD

Listen to a short conversation and answer the three questions below.

7. What kind of vacation does the man want to take?   Ⓐ Ⓑ Ⓒ Ⓓ
   (A) A tour of Australia
   (B) A camping vacation
   (C) A vacation in a remote place
   (D) A week by the ocean

8. What does the woman prefer?
   (A) Adventure trips
   (B) Comfortable vacations
   (C) Being close to nature
   (D) Staying at home

9. Why does the woman become interested in the man's suggestion?
   (A) He tells her they will take a world tour.
   (B) He tells her they will go to Australia.
   (C) He tells her they will stay in a high-class hotel.
   (D) He tells her the lodges are remote but comfortable.

Part 4 Short Talk

Listen to a short talk and answer the three questions below.

10. Who can apply for the space adventure?
    (A) Anyone who wants to.
    (B) Anyone who has enough money.
    (C) Anyone working at the International Space Station.
    (D) Those who pass the tests.

11. What is included in the adventure holiday?
    (A) Medical training.
    (B) A tour of Moscow.
    (C) A medical examination.
    (D) Prize money.

12. What is a major drawback?
    (A) The cost.
    (B) Having to go into space.
    (C) Having to stay at the International Space Station.
    (D) The adventure.

Human Cloning: Do We Need It?

LISTENING PRACTICE

A. Warm-up Activity I: Vocabulary and Phrases

Choose the correct meaning for the following words or phrases from (1) to (12).

( ) beneficial ( ) chores ( ) ban
( ) manipulate ( ) preserve ( ) endangered species
( ) know where (someone's) coming from ( ) organ
( ) infertile couple ( ) pros and cons ( ) take over
( ) Sounds good.

(1) to control or influence 〜を操作する (2) part of the body that has a particular function 臓器 (3) arguments for and against something 賛否両論 (4) having a helpful or useful effect 有益な (5) tasks (usually household) that you usually do 日常の定期的な雑用 (6) to forbid something officially 禁止する (7) kinds of plants or animals at risk of dying out 絶滅寸前の種 (8) to keep something alive or safe from danger 保存する, 保護する (9) a husband and wife who are unable to have children 不妊症の夫婦 (10) I agree. それはいいね (11) to understand what someone means or feels 言っていることが分かる (12) to get control of something 乗っ取る

B. Warm-up Activity II

If you agree with the following ideas, write A (=agree). If you don't, write D (=disagree).

1. Human cloning is beneficial because it can save people's lives.   ( )
2. I want to have a clone to help me do my chores.   ( )
3. Human cloning must be banned because we should not manipulate life.   ( )
4. We ought to preserve endangered animals by using cloning technology.   ( )
5. Because we die, we feel that life has value, and thus we can live well.   ( )

Listening Practice

Listen to the conversation and fill in the blanks. Then practice reading with a partner.

At a coffee shop

Atsushi: I have so many things to do! _____, reports, reading. How am I supposed to do all that and _____ at the same time! What I need is another _____!

Larry: I know where you're coming from! If there was another me, I could get a lot more things done. But I guess we'll have to wait for human clones to be _____.

Atsushi: Maybe cloning shouldn't be banned. Did you know that it can be used to preserve endangered species and even to _____ organs and human skin? It can save lives!

Phil: I've heard that it can help infertile couples have children.

Larry: Of course, there are pros and cons on cloning, just like any _____ topic.

Phil: Yeah. What if you did have another you? He could help you with your homework and do your job for you, but what about your _____ with people? Your girlfriend might be kissing him. Yuck!

Larry: He might even try to control you. He could take over your life.

Atsushi: You watch too many movies.

Larry: You're probably _____. And speaking of movies, "The Clone" is _____ at the theater now. Let's go see it.

Atsushi: Sounds good.

Larry: Let's go!

Listen to the CD and write the questions. Then listen to the conversation again and answer the questions.

1. _____

2. _____

3. _____

4. _____

Reading and Writing Practice

A. Words and Phrases

foundation 財団　　benefits 利点　　dinosaur 恐竜　　tolerate 容認する　　kidney 腎臓　　numerous 多数の　　argument 論拠　　allow 認める　　research 研究　　lead up to ～に通じる　　freedom 自由　　tolerance 寛容さ　　view 考え方　　infertility 不妊症　　treatment 治療　　go through 経験する　　painful 痛みを伴う　　procedure 処置　　run out of 使い果たす　　liver 肝臓　　transplant 移植

B. True-False Questions

Read the questions below, and then read the following passage to find the answers.

1. The Human Cloning Foundation shows some of the benefits of human cloning on its Web site.　　T / F
2. In the future we'll be able to preserve any species except dinosaurs.　　T / F
3. Most Americans agree that they need guns to protect themselves.　　T / F
4. In a free society we should not tolerate ideas that we don't agree with.　　T / F
5. With cloning, childless people could have their DNA continue to exist on earth.　T / F
6. With cloning, infertile couples could have children with less physical and mental pain.　　T / F
7. Cloning technology could be used to create livers and kidneys, but not hearts.　T / F

C. Let's Read!

The Human Cloning Foundation (http://www.humancloning.org/benefits.php and http://www.humancloning.org/allthe.php) mentions numerous situations in which it believes cloning can be beneficial. Some of them are given below. Do you think they are strong or weak arguments for allowing cloning?

1 Endangered species could be saved

Through the research leading up to human cloning, we will perfect the technology to clone animals, and thus we can forever preserve endangered species, as well as human beings.

2 We believe in freedom

Freedom sometimes means having tolerance for others and their beliefs. In America, for example, some people believe in gun control and some don't. Some people believe in one religion and others in another. In a free society we know that we must tolerate some views that we don't agree with so that we all may be free. For this reason human cloning should be allowed.

3 We could live on through a later-born twin

Some childless people feel that by being cloned, their later-born twin (clone) would help them or their DNA to live on in the same sense that people who have children live on.

4 Infertility

With cloning, infertile couples could have children. Current infertility treatments are less than 10 percent successful. Couples go through physically and emotionally painful procedures for a small chance of having children. Many couples run out of time and money without successfully having children. Human cloning could make it possible for many more infertile couples to have children than ever before.

5 Organ failure (Organ implants)
We may be able to clone livers, kidneys, hearts etc. for transplants.   (240 words)

D Summarizing

Read the paragraph again and write appropriate words or phrases in the spaces.

Based on _____ on cloning, we will be able to clone animals in the future, and thus we can preserve _____, as well as human beings, forever.

We have to tolerate _____ and their _____. For example, some people may _____ gun control and some may not. But in a _____ we should tolerate some _____ that we _____ with in order to keep our _____.

Some people who have no _____ could have themselves _____, and their _____ could carry on _____ after they die.

Infertile couples _____ with cloning technology. Current infertility treatments are not very _____. Many couples do not succeed in having children before running _____. With the technology of _____, many _____ infertile couples could have children _____.

E Speaking/Writing

1. What are your views on human cloning?

2. Should cloning of living things other than humans be allowed?

Preparation for the TOEIC® TEST

Unit 5

Part 1 — Photographs

Look at each picture and listen to four statements. Choose the statement that best describes each picture.

1. Ⓐ Ⓑ Ⓒ Ⓓ

2. Ⓐ Ⓑ Ⓒ Ⓓ

Part 2 — Question-Response

Listen to a question followed by three responses and then choose the best response.

3. Mark your answer on your answer sheet.   Ⓐ Ⓑ Ⓒ
4. Mark your answer on your answer sheet.   Ⓐ Ⓑ Ⓒ
5. Mark your answer on your answer sheet.   Ⓐ Ⓑ Ⓒ
6. Mark your answer on your answer sheet.   Ⓐ Ⓑ Ⓒ

Part 3 — Short Conversation

Listen to a short conversation and answer the three questions below.

7. Why does the woman not use an air-conditioner?   Ⓐ Ⓑ Ⓒ Ⓓ
   (A) She does not have one.
   (B) It is broken.
   (C) It is too expensive.
   (D) It makes her sick.

8. When does the man use his air-conditioner? Ⓐ Ⓑ Ⓒ Ⓓ
   (A) Only in the daytime
   (B) Only at night
   (C) Hardly ever
   (D) Whenever he is home

9. What does the woman do if she feels hot? Ⓐ Ⓑ Ⓒ Ⓓ
   (A) She opens a window.
   (B) She uses a fan.
   (C) She goes out.
   (D) She has a cold drink.

Part 4 Short Talk

Listen to a short talk and answer the three questions below.

10. What is the speaker doing? Ⓐ Ⓑ Ⓒ Ⓓ
    (A) She is saying how jealous she is.
    (B) She is gossiping.
    (C) She is pretending she is not interested.
    (D) She is seeking information from the public.

11. What does the speaker say about Richard? Ⓐ Ⓑ Ⓒ Ⓓ
    (A) She thinks he has charm.
    (B) She thinks he is just like Jane.
    (C) She thinks he isn't very active.
    (D) She thinks he eats so many potatoes he looks like one.

12. What does she think Jane and Richard should do? Ⓐ Ⓑ Ⓒ Ⓓ
    (A) Have children.
    (B) Get back together again.
    (C) Separate for good.
    (D) Do more things on their own instead of together.

Unit 6

Your Culture or Mine?

LISTENING PRACTICE

A. Warm-up Activity I: Vocabulary and Phrases

Choose the correct meaning for the following words or phrases from (1) to (10).

( ) aspect ( ) participate in ( ) ethnic
( ) be supposed to ( ) bother ( ) separate
( ) related to ( ) superficial ( ) aisle
( ) priest

(1) person who performs religious duties or ceremonies 司祭　　(2) connected with ～と関係を持った　　(3) obvious, on the surface only 表面的な　　(4) a particular part or feature of a situation, idea, etc. 側面　　(5) connected with a nation, race, or tribe that shares a cultural tradition 民族の　　(6) to become involved in ～に参加する　　(7) to divide into different parts 切り離す　　(8) to annoy, worry, or upset 困らせる，悩ませる　　(9) to think that something is probably true ～だと思われている　　(10) passage between rows of seats in a church, theater, train, etc. 座席の間の通路

B. Warm-up Activity II

1. Which aspects of Japan's traditional culture are you interested in?
2. Have you studied any traditional Japanese arts?
3. Which aspects of Japanese culture do you think would be most difficult to explain to a non-Japanese?
4. How do you feel when you see non-Japanese participating in some aspect of Japanese culture (for example, doing kendo or tea ceremony)?
5. Are you interested in learning the traditional culture of some other country or ethnic group?

C. Listening Practice

Listen to the conversation and fill in the blanks. Then practice reading with a partner.

Manuel: You know, I saw something interesting on TV the other night. They showed a big *bon* dance _____ in Malaysia, with 20 or 30 thousand people participating. It was supposed to be the biggest in the world.

Yuriko: In Malaysia?

Manuel: Yes. Japanese people who live in the _____ were taking part, of course, but most of the people dancing were young Malaysians. Some were even _____ *yukata*, although they weren't all wearing them in the Japanese way.

Yuriko: Well, if they enjoyed themselves, I suppose it's all right, but still, the idea bothers me a little. *Bon odori* are part of traditional Japanese culture, and if you separate them from the _____ of the culture and make them a kind of entertainment, something is lost.

Manuel: I see your point. Maybe the Malaysians didn't understand the religious beliefs and customs related to *obon* and were _____ enjoying the superficial aspects.

Yuriko: Anyway, I've been wanting to show you the pictures from my sister's wedding. Here, isn't she beautiful?

Manuel: Yes, she's very pretty. But it looks like she's in _____. I didn't know your family is Christian.

Yuriko: Oh, we're not. But a Christian wedding ceremony is so romantic, don't you _____? Walking down the aisle, the organ playing, the priest in his robes,…

Manuel: And you're _____ about *bon odori* in Malaysia?

Listen to the CD and write the questions. Then listen to the conversation again and answer the questions.

1. _____

2. _____

3. _____

4. _____

5. _____

Reading and Writing Practice

A Words and Phrases

intellectual property 知的財産   patent 特許   imitate まねる   solve（問題などを）解決する   own 所有する   determine 決定する   invention 発明   ownership 所有権   establish 確立する   copyright 著作権   author 著者   individual 一人一人の   similar to ～に似た   tattoo 入れ墨   state 意見を述べる   Maori-inspired マオリ文化からヒントを得た   reproduction 複製   minority group 少数派   developing country 発展途上国   seek 探し求める   exploitation 利益目的の利用   in response これに対応して   clarify 明確にする   privilege 特別な権利   isolate 孤立化させる   thereby それによって   dying out 絶滅   ingredient 食材   insist on 強く主張する

B True-False Questions

Read the questions below, and then read the following passage to find the answers.

1. Intellectual property includes things such as cars and houses.   T / F
2. Patents are a way of protecting intellectual property.   T / F
3. Tattoos are a part of traditional Maori culture.   T / F
4. The Maori don't mind if other people imitate their culture.   T / F
5. The World Intellectual Property Organization is interested in traditional culture.   T / F
6. Treating traditional culture as intellectual property would solve the problem.   T / F
7. Sushi is popular in only a few countries outside Japan.   T / F

C Let's Read!

Traditional Culture as Intellectual Property

Property is usually thought of as something physical, such as land, a house, or a car, and deciding who owns it is not so difficult. In recent years, however, much attention has been given to *intellectual* property, and determining who owns *it* can be much more complicated. Intellectual property is a result of human creativity, such as a work of literature or art, an invention, or a commercial design. Ownership of this kind of property is established by patent and copyright laws. An author, for example, has the right to control the copying and use of material he or she has written. But what about creations of the mind that do not belong to individual people?

One example of this can be seen in connection with a game for Sony's popular PlayStation 2. *The Mark of Kri* features a larger-than-life hero with markings similar to the traditional tattoos of the Maori people of New Zealand. The company's advertising, in fact, states that the violent video is "set in a Maori-inspired world."* Some Maori have criticized Sony, not only for using Maori images incorrectly but also for trying to make a profit by using traditional Maori culture without having any right to do so. They claim that their traditional culture, including tattoos and even language, is a form of intellectual property and that they have the right to control its use or reproduction.

Increasingly, minority ethnic groups and developing countries are seeking ways to protect their traditional culture and knowledge from commercial exploitation by developed countries. In response, the World Intellectual Property Organization has been trying to clarify the relationship of intellectual property and expressions of traditional culture.

The importance of protecting such expressions is acknowledged by many, but there are also problems related to giving ownership of intellectual property to groups. If people who are not members of a group want to use some aspect of its traditional culture, should they have to pay for that privilege? If so, who receives the payment? Moreover, such a system could have a negative effect on the group by isolating the culture and thereby increasing the possibility of its dying out.

Take sushi, for example. This Japanese food is now enjoying great popularity around the world. Many Japanese might be shocked at some of the ingredients that are combined under the name of "sushi," but if they begin charging non-Japanese sushi makers for the right to sell their creations or insisting on only traditional ingredients, we might all be the losers. Surely part of the value of a culture lies in sharing it with others. (433 words)

D Summarizing

Read the paragraph again and write appropriate words or phrases in the spaces.

Intellectual property consists of the results of _____, rather than physical things such as _____. _____ of intellectual property is established by _____ and _____. Authors, for example, can control _____ and _____ of their _____ through copyrights.

A character in a game for _____ has markings similar to _____ of the Maori. Some Maori object not only because the images are used _____ but also because people who have no _____ to use Maori culture are making a

_____ from it.

Complaints of commercial exploitation of traditional culture are often made by minority ethnic groups or _____ against _____. The World Intellectual Property Organization is trying to _____ the relationship of _____ and _____.

Giving ownership of _____ to groups could cause problems, such as deciding whether people must _____ for the _____ of using cultural images and who would receive _____. It could also isolate _____ and increase _____.

_____ is an example of _____ culture that is popular _____. Sometimes it is made with _____ that would surprise _____, but if non-Japanese _____ were restricted, we might all lose out on an interesting food experience. It seems that we need to _____ our culture _____.

E Speaking/Writing

1. Which aspect of traditional Japanese culture are you most interested in? Why?

2. Do you think ethnic groups or countries should copyright their traditional culture? Why or why not?

Preparation for the TOEIC® TEST

Unit 6

Part 1 — Photographs

Look at each picture and listen to four statements. Choose the statement that best describes each picture.

1.

Ⓐ Ⓑ Ⓒ Ⓓ

2.

Ⓐ Ⓑ Ⓒ Ⓓ

Part 2 — Question-Response

Listen to a question followed by three responses and then choose the best response.

3. Mark your answer on your answer sheet.   Ⓐ Ⓑ Ⓒ
4. Mark your answer on your answer sheet.   Ⓐ Ⓑ Ⓒ
5. Mark your answer on your answer sheet.   Ⓐ Ⓑ Ⓒ
6. Mark your answer on your answer sheet.   Ⓐ Ⓑ Ⓒ

Part 3 — Short Conversation

Listen to a short conversation and answer the three questions below.

7. What has the women recently done?   Ⓐ Ⓑ Ⓒ Ⓓ
   (A) Gone to Hawaii
   (B) Started a new hobby
   (C) Booked a vacation
   (D) Caught a cold

8. What does the woman say about surfing? Ⓐ Ⓑ Ⓒ Ⓓ
   (A) It is difficult and dangerous.
   (B) It is dangerous but not difficult.
   (C) It is difficult but not dangerous.
   (D) It is neither dangerous nor difficult.

9. What do we learn about the man? Ⓐ Ⓑ Ⓒ Ⓓ
   (A) He likes outdoor activities.
   (B) He prefers England to Hawaii.
   (C) He likes good food and wine.
   (D) He would rather be inside than outside.

Part 4 — Short Talk

Listen to a short talk and answer the three questions below.

10. What is the purpose of this talk? Ⓐ Ⓑ Ⓒ Ⓓ
    (A) To inform people about the history of space.
    (B) To request information about eclipses.
    (C) To tell a story.
    (D) To announce a competition.

11. Why does the speaker mention the fires of the sun going out? Ⓐ Ⓑ Ⓒ Ⓓ
    (A) He is explaining why eclipses happen.
    (B) He is asking people to give explanations of eclipses.
    (C) He is explaining what people believed in the past.
    (D) He is predicting the future.

12. What does he say about the book on the moon and the stars? Ⓐ Ⓑ Ⓒ Ⓓ
    (A) The book is full of fantastic stories.
    (B) The book explains why eclipses happen.
    (C) The book is a surprise.
    (D) The book will be given as a prize.

Unit 7

City Food from Field to Table

LISTENING PRACTICE

A. Warm-up Activity I: Vocabulary and Phrases

Choose the correct meaning for the following words or phrases from (1) to (10).

(　) price　　　　　　(　) agricultural chemical　　(　) supper
(　) soybean　　　　　(　) budget　　　　　　　　(　) residual
(　) environment　　　(　) fossil fuel　　　　　　　(　) preach
(　) authentic

(1) fuel such as coal or oil that was formed from the remains of plants or animals 化石燃料　　(2) remaining 残留性の　　(3) genuine, not a copy 本物の　　(4) the natural world in which we live 自然環境　　(5) the money available to a person to use for living expenses 家計，生活費　　(6) the amount of money you have to pay for something 値段　　(7) type of bean that is high in protein 大豆　　(8) chemicals used in agriculture to protect crops from pests, disease, or unwanted plants 農薬　　(9) to give advice about behavior, morals, etc. 熱心に説く　　(10) the evening meal 夕食

B. Warm-up Activity II

1. Do you prefer to prepare meals at home or to eat out?
2. Where do you usually buy food? Why?
3. Do you pay attention to where the food you buy was grown?
4. Are you more concerned about the price of food or the place where it was grown?
5. Are you concerned about agricultural chemicals on your food?

Listening Practice

Listen to the conversation and fill in the blanks. Then practice reading with a partner.

At the supermarket

Yoshikazu: Hi, Jae-hwan. What's _____ supper tonight?

Jae-hwan: Kimchi soup. I want to put tofu in it, but I can't find any made _____ soybeans grown in Japan.

Yoshikazu: What _____ does that make? Soybeans are soybeans, aren't they?

Jae-hwan: I always try to buy food grown as _____ to home as possible. How about the things in your basket?

Yoshikazu: Hmmm, let's see. These kiwi fruit are from New Zealand, the cherries from the U.S., the beef from Australia. Shiitake are Japanese food, though, so I'm sure… oh, they're from China. Anyway, these were all the _____ of each item.

Jae-hwan: On our student budgets, _____ money *is* important, but aren't you concerned about eating foods from so far away?

Yoshikazu: Well, I *have* heard that foods from other countries have residual chemicals _____ them.

Jae-hwan: Sometimes they do, and that's bad for your health, but imported food is also bad for the health of the environment. Think of _____ the fossil fuel that's used to bring it here.

Yoshikazu: You're probably right. OK, I'll try to do better. Say, you _____ practice what you preach. This kimchi is from Korea.

Jae-hwan: Well, sometimes "authentic" _____ more important than "local."

Listen to the CD and write the questions. Then listen to the conversation again and answer the questions.

1. _____

2. _____

3. _____

4. _____

Reading and Writing Practice

A Words and Phrases

food security 食料の安定確保　　empty lot 空地　　urban 都市部の　　fade だんだんなくなる
Ministry of Agriculture, Forestry and Fisheries 農林水産省　　in succession 連続して
self-sufficiency rate 自給率　　supplier 供給者　　unrest 不安　　disaster 災害
drought 長期的水不足　　secure 確保する　　suspicion 疑い　　embargo 禁止
ally 同盟国　　collapse 崩壊する　　nutritional 栄養の　　shortage 不足　　domestic 国内の
reduction 削減　　tear down 〜を取り壊す　　unavailability 入手不能　　organic 有機農法を使った　　reliant on 〜を頼みにした　　oxen 雄牛　　intensive 集約的な　　staple 主要な

B True-False Questions

Read the questions below, and then read the following passage to find the answers.

1. Japan imports 40% of its food.　　　　　　　　　　　　　　　　　T / F
2. Some people worry that Japan has a food security problem.　　　　T / F
3. Cuba is slightly larger in area than Japan.　　　　　　　　　　　　T / F
4. Cuba imports much of its food from the United States.　　　　　　T / F
5. People in Havana grow food in backyards and empty lots.　　　　　T / F
6. Animals are not used in farming in Cuba because they are too slow.　T / F
7. Urban agriculture in Cuba may fade if trade conditions improve.　　T / F

C Let's Read!

　Every year the Japanese Ministry of Agriculture, Forestry and Fisheries publishes a White Paper on the state of agriculture in Japan, and for several years in succession, it has stressed that Japan's food self-sufficiency rate, in terms of the calorie base, is about 40%. In other words, 60% of the calories eaten in Japan come from imported food. In a time of peace, when Japan's suppliers are not experiencing production problems, this does not seem to be a serious problem, but people concerned about "food security" think it's a dangerous number.

　During a war or other political unrest or during natural disasters such as drought, Japan might have trouble securing the food it needs. Many people seem to think that because Japan is a small country with little agricultural land, it must rely on imported food. The example of another small country, however, shows that other things *can* be done.

　Cuba, a country 110,922km² in area (about half the size of Honshū), became the target of American anger and suspicion when Fidel Castro led a successful revolution there and established a communist government. From 1960 a U.S. trade embargo caused Cuba to rely mainly on its ally, the Soviet Union, for many of its needs, including food. At the same time, a large portion of farmland was given over to the production of sugar, most of which was exported, and agriculture was dependent on chemicals and large machinery.

When the Soviet Union collapsed in 1991, Cuba lost a major source of food and chemicals, and the population faced serious nutritional shortages. A major effort was begun to improve Cuban agriculture and increase domestic production. Along with a reduction in large-scale farming for export, an emphasis was put on urban agriculture. In the capital city of Havana, backyards and empty lots were turned into gardens. Old factories were torn down and made into farms. In part because of the unavailability of chemicals, but also for health reasons, urban agriculture had to be organic and reliant on natural pest control. Animals such as horses and oxen were sometimes used instead of tractors to save fuel.

The result has been more successful than most people expected. In 2003 a minimum of 300 grams of fruit and vegetables a day for each person in Havana was grown within the city limits. Research on intensive farming methods was suggesting the possibility of self-sufficiency in the staple food of rice in the future. Of course, this experiment was born of necessity, not choice, and as Cuba's international trade situation improves, the energy put into achieving food self-sufficiency may fade. Nevertheless, Cuba has presented an excellent picture of what can be done.

(446 words)

D Summarizing

Read the paragraph again and write appropriate words or phrases in the spaces.

A document published by the Japanese Government _____ reminds the Japanese that they import _____. As long as there is _____ and other countries do not have _____, this may not be a problem, but some people are worried about _____.

If there is a war or political unrest or a natural disaster occurs, Japan could have trouble _____. Many people seem to think that the only solution is to _____, but something else can be done.

Cuba, a country _____ than Japan, suffers from _____ by the United States. Because of this it used to get much of what it needed, including food, from the Soviet Union. Also, much farmland was devoted to production of _____ for _____.

When the _____ collapsed, Cuba experienced shortages of _____ and _____. It cut back on _____ and increased _____. In Havana many places have been turned into _____ and _____. Farming there is _____ and sometimes _____.

Havana's urban agriculture can supply at least _____ _____. Self-sufficiency in _____ may be possible in the future. As conditions change, Cuba's self-sufficiency effort may _____, but it is a good example of _____.

◆E◆ Speaking/Writing

1. What can Japan do to improve its food security?

2. Are you interested in gardening or farming?

Preparation for the TOEIC® TEST

Unit 7

Part 1 — Photographs

Look at each picture and listen to four statements. Choose the statement that best describes each picture.

1. Ⓐ Ⓑ Ⓒ Ⓓ

2. Ⓐ Ⓑ Ⓒ Ⓓ

Part 2 — Question-Response

Listen to a question followed by three responses and then choose the best response.

3. Mark your answer on your answer sheet. Ⓐ Ⓑ Ⓒ
4. Mark your answer on your answer sheet. Ⓐ Ⓑ Ⓒ
5. Mark your answer on your answer sheet. Ⓐ Ⓑ Ⓒ
6. Mark your answer on your answer sheet. Ⓐ Ⓑ Ⓒ

Part 3 — Short Conversation

Listen to a short conversation and answer the three questions below.

7. How much will the usual printing company charge?   Ⓐ Ⓑ Ⓒ Ⓓ
    (A) $1,600
    (B) $2,000
    (C) $3,000
    (D) $5,000

8. How does the company in Singapore compare with the usual company? Ⓐ Ⓑ Ⓒ Ⓓ
    (A) It is cheaper and quicker.
    (B) It is cheaper and slower.
    (C) It is quicker and more expensive.
    (D) It is more expensive and slower.

9. What does the woman want to do? Ⓐ Ⓑ Ⓒ Ⓓ
    (A) Use the usual company
    (B) Use the Singaporean company
    (C) Ask more questions
    (D) Go to visit the Singaporean company

Part 4 — Short Talk

Listen to a short talk and answer the three questions below.

10. What was the joystick first used for? Ⓐ Ⓑ Ⓒ Ⓓ
    (A) Airplanes.
    (B) Computers.
    (C) Cell phones.
    (D) Game controllers.

11. Who invented the joystick? Ⓐ Ⓑ Ⓒ Ⓓ
    (A) No-one has any idea about its origins.
    (B) Probably an aviator called Robert Esnault-Peltrie.
    (C) A computer engineer.
    (D) A machine translator.

12. Why is the joystick a successful input device? Ⓐ Ⓑ Ⓒ Ⓓ
    (A) Computers and game controllers sell well.
    (B) It is simple, efficient and easy to control.
    (C) It brings joy to many people.
    (D) It allows airplanes to easily be controlled.

Unit 8

The Making of a Nobel Prize-winner

LISTENING PRACTICE

A. Warm-up Activity I: Vocabulary and Phrases

Choose the correct meaning for the following words or phrases from (1) to (12).

(　　) study abroad　　(　　) internship　　(　　) latest
(　　) bulletin board　(　　) scholarship　　(　　) expenses
(　　) major　　　　　(　　) utilize　　　　(　　) practical
(　　) nationwide　　　(　　) usefulness　　 (　　) apply for

(1)to make a formal request for something, usually in writing 申し込む　　(2)the quality of being possible to use 有用性　　(3)the most recent or newest 最新の　　(4)connected with real situations 実践的な　　(5)student specializing in a particular subject 専攻生　　(6)to use something, especially for a practical purpose 利用する　　(7)work in a company, etc. as a form of training 企業実習　　(8)money spent for a particular purpose 費用　　(9)a board for putting notices on 掲示板　　(10)money given to someone by an organization to help pay for their education 奨学金　　(11)to pursue one's education in a foreign country 留学する　　(12)happening in all parts of a country 全国規模の

B. Warm-up Activity II

1. Would you like to study abroad?
2. Do you want to do an internship before you graduate from the university?
3. Which do you think is a better way to learn—study or experience?
4. What do you think is the best way to learn English?
5. Why have there been so few Nobel Prize-winners from Japan?

47

Listening Practice

Listen to the conversation and fill in the blanks. Then practice reading with a partner.

John: Kazue, did you know that the university is looking for first-year students to study _____ during summer vacation? It's a special program that will start next year.

Kazue: I haven't heard anything about it. How do you always get the latest information so quickly, John?

John: I always look at the university bulletin board very _____. The other day I read that we can get a special scholarship for this program. It will pay almost two-thirds of the expenses. What do you think?

Kazue: Is it for English study? I'm not interested in an _____ English program. I'm not an English major.

John: No. It's a kind of combination program. You take both English classes and science seminars, and you can visit several research centers and _____ utilizing the latest scientific theories and technologies.

Kazue: That sounds interesting *and* practical. We can see how science is being used to make real _____.

John: That's the point. The program's slogan is "See and experience the real world while you are young!" The new university president believes that students should experience the real world soon after they enter the university because it will make them more _____ to study. He's also planning to start a system of nationwide internships for first-year students.

Kazue: That's a good idea. If we don't know what's going on in the real workplace, we won't have a clear idea of the knowledge, skills, and _____ we need for the jobs we want. Necessity is also the mother of "serious study." We usually can't feel the importance and usefulness of what we're studying from books and lectures _____.

John: I'm going to apply for the study abroad program. You're interested too, aren't you?

Kazue: Of course. I'll go and get the application form right _____. But did you check about whether you can apply for an international exchange program? Remember, you're _____ an exchange student *here*.

John: Gee, I forgot about that.

Listen to the CD and write the questions. Then listen to the conversation again and answer the questions.

1. _____

_____

2. _____
_____
3. _____
_____
4. _____
_____

READING AND WRITING PRACTICE

A Words and Phrases

graduate student 大学院生　　emphasize 強調する　　long-term 長期的な　　suggestion 提案　　fortunate 幸運な　　share 共有する　　broaden 広める　　view ものの見方　　influence 影響を与える　　acknowledge 認める　　make progress 進歩する　　competitive 競争的な　　recently 最近　　developed country 先進国　　physics 物理学　　confident 自信のある　　praise 賞賛する　　inferior 劣った　　bash 強く批判する　　profit 利益　　adjust 手を加える　　responsibility 責任　　recognize 認識する　　benefit 利益をもたらす　　intellectual 知的な　　property 財産　　generation 世代　　minister 大臣　　reward 報奨金を与える　　contribute to 〜に貢献する　　require 要求する　　experiment 実験する　　essential 必要な　　achieve 達成する　　blossom 咲く　　seed 種　　pursue 追い求める

B True-False Questions

Read the questions below, and then read the following passage to find the answers.

1. Professor Koshiba went to the U.S. as an undergraduate student.　　T / F
2. Professor Koshiba could not speak English at all when he first went to the U.S.　　T / F
3. The Japanese government has emphasized support for long-term research.　　T / F
4. Professor Koshiba has three suggestions for making children more interested in science.　　T / F
5. Professor Koshiba thinks that the Japanese government should give scholarships to graduate students.　　T / F

C Let's Read!

Interview with Nobel Prize-winner Masatoshi Koshiba

Interviewer: Tell me about your experience when you went to the U.S. as a graduate student.

Koshiba: At that time (1953), studying abroad was like a dream come true, so I was very fortunate. At first I couldn't speak the language at all, but I shared a room with an Australian student, and I needed to use English to communicate. After a while, I got used to it. I want to tell young people that, if possible, it's better to go while you are young. It's easier not only to learn the language quickly, but also to broaden your views.

Interviewer: What did you learn most from living abroad?

Koshiba: What influenced me most was that American students didn't hesitate to speak out. Students would stand up and point out a speaker's mistake, even if it was a speech by a Nobel Prize-winning professor. In Japan, though, that would be considered rude. No matter whose opinion it is, acknowledging that what's right is right is necessary for making progress in the severely competitive academic world. But recently, I find Japanese students are able to compete on the same level as students from any other developed country, at least in the field of physics.

Interviewer: So you think we ought to be more confident about ourselves?

Koshiba: Yes, instead of noticing good things about ourselves only after being praised overseas—which is the way it is now. Perhaps we feel inferior about doing basic research, and we believe it when the foreign press bashes our country, saying Japan makes commercial profit by slightly adjusting the findings of others. Also, our government has been putting too much importance on increasing economic strength, while forgetting its responsibility to support long-term research. A civilized country is one that recognizes value in benefiting the common intellectual property of humankind.

Interviewer: What do you think the government can do for future generations?

Koshiba: When I met with the education minister, I made three suggestions for making children more interested in science. One is rewarding junior high science teachers who contribute to this purpose. We can measure their progress by asking students at the beginning and the end of the school year about their love of science. Another idea is to require graduate students studying physics to teach at junior high schools in return for government scholarships. Only teachers who enjoy science can tell kids about the fun of it. The third suggestion is to build more science museums where children can experiment with their own hands, instead of just looking at big dinosaur bones.

Interviewer: Finally, what is the essential factor for achieving internationally recognized success?

Koshiba: Why would anybody make an effort if there was an answer to that?! But one thing I believe is that you can't make a flower blossom without a seed, or without keeping what I call an "egg of dreams." I kept pursuing my dream with all my strength.   (490 words; first published as "Masatoshi Koshiba: The Nobelist Who Keeps the Eggs of His Dreams," *English Zone*, no. 1, January 2003.)

D Summarizing

Read the paragraph again and write appropriate words or phrases in the spaces.

When Dr. Koshiba went _____, he wasn't able to speak English, but he soon _____. Based on his experience, he thinks young people should _____ while they are young.

The most important thing he learned from living abroad was that American students _____. Students in the U.S. _____ _____, but in Japan _____ rude. Nevertheless, it is necessary to _____. Recently, though, Japanese students are able to do this on _____ _____.

Dr. Koshiba thinks that the Japanese should not wait until _____ to notice _____. They are too likely to feel _____ _____ and to believe criticism from the foreign press. Also, the government has emphasized _____ rather than _____ _____. As a civilized nation, Japan should recognize _____ _____.

One thing that can be done to get children interested in science is to reward _____ _____. Also, graduate students in physics should be required to _____ _____ in return _____. A final suggestion is to build _____.

While Dr. Koshiba can't say what is the essential factor for achieving international success, he believes that we should have _____. In other words, we should keep _____.

E Speaking/Writing

1. If you could study abroad, where and what would you like to study? Why?

2. Do you think it's a serious problem that Japan doesn't produce many Nobel Prize-winners? Why or why not?

Preparation for the TOEIC® TEST

Unit 8

Part 1 — Photographs

Look at each picture and listen to four statements. Choose the statement that best describes each picture.

1. Ⓐ Ⓑ Ⓒ Ⓓ

2. Ⓐ Ⓑ Ⓒ Ⓓ

Part 2 — Question-Response

Listen to a question followed by three responses and then choose the best response.

3. Mark your answer on your answer sheet. Ⓐ Ⓑ Ⓒ

4. Mark your answer on your answer sheet. Ⓐ Ⓑ Ⓒ

5. Mark your answer on your answer sheet. Ⓐ Ⓑ Ⓒ

6. Mark your answer on your answer sheet. Ⓐ Ⓑ Ⓒ

Part 3 — Short Conversation

Listen to a short conversation and answer the three questions below.

7. What did the woman enjoy most about her vacation? Ⓐ Ⓑ Ⓒ Ⓓ
    (A) Seeing many animals
    (B) The African scenery
    (C) Getting up early
    (D) Riding in a balloon

8. What kind of animal does the woman NOT mention?
   (A) Lion
   (B) Zebra
   (C) Antelope
   (D) Buffalo

9. What did the woman say about the balloon ride?
   (A) She was scared.
   (B) It started at 3 a.m.
   (C) She wants to take it up.
   (D) It was a great experience.

Part 4 — Short Talk

Listen to a short talk and answer the three questions below.

10. When was the first European Astronomy Symposium held?
    (A) Late September.
    (B) At the Palace Convention Center.
    (C) Every year.
    (D) Eight years ago.

11. What extra events will be held?
    (A) A special closing night dinner.
    (B) A formal dinner on the first night of the conference.
    (C) Guest speakers.
    (D) Online registration.

12. What will happen at the Symposium?
    (A) Presentations will be given in all European languages.
    (B) There will be a guest speaker from Luxembourg.
    (C) There will be two guest speakers.
    (D) There will be at least two guest speakers.

Unit 9

Walking for Health: Yours and the Earth's

LISTENING PRACTICE

A Warm-up Activity I: Vocabulary and Phrases

Choose the correct meaning for the following words or phrases from (1) to (16).

(　) public transportation　(　) global warming　(　) on foot
(　) air pollution　(　) environment-conscious　(　) policy
(　) carbon dioxide　(　) emission
(　) be concerned about　(　) obesity　(　) heart attack
(　) stroke　(　) diabetes　(　) contribute to
(　) depend on　(　) executive

(1) to be one of the causes of something 〜の一因となる　(2) to rely on 〜に依存する　(3) an agreed upon plan of action 方針　(4) system for carrying people from one place to another using vehicles 公共交通機関　(5) dirty air 空気汚染　(6) extreme fatness 肥満　(7) person with an important position in a company 重役, 経営幹部　(8) illness caused when a blood vessel in the brain bursts or is blocked 脳卒中　(9) gas, etc. that is sent into the air 排出ガス　(10) gas produced by burning carbon 二酸化炭素　(11) particularly aware of or interested in the natural environment 環境を意識した　(12) medical condition caused by a lack of insulin 糖尿病　(13) by walking 歩いて　(14) serious medical condition that occurs when the heart stops working normally 心臓発作　(15) increase in the temperature of the earth's atmosphere 地球温暖化　(16) to have a strong interest in 〜に関心を持つ

B Warm-up Activity II

1. How do you come to the university?
2. Do you often use public transportation?

3. Is there anything that you do regularly to protect your health?
4. What's the best way to control your weight?
5. What's the main reason for global warming?

Listening Practice

Listen to the conversation and fill in the blanks. Then practice reading with a partner.

Junji: Good morning, Vikram.
Vikram: Good morning, Junji. You're on _____ today. Is something wrong with your car?
Junji: No. Today is "No Car Day" at my company.
Vikram: "No Car Day"? What's that? I've never heard of it.
Junji: Well, our company is developing products for _____ air pollution, so we have to be very environment-conscious. The company has a policy that twice a week we don't come to work by car, in order to _____ carbon dioxide emissions. On "No Car Day" we have to walk or use public _____.
Vikram: That's great. Global warming is a big problem, and they say that carbon dioxide emissions are the _____ cause. Your company really is concerned about the environment.
Junji: And walking is good for your health too. It's good exercise.
Vikram: _____ true. Obesity is a big problem in the U.S., and more and more people have weight-related diseases like heart attack, stroke and diabetes. _____ of exercise contributes to obesity, and depending on cars _____ people to exercise even less.
Junji: Is it true that people in the U.S. who are overweight or who _____ can't get promoted?
Vikram: I've heard that it may happen. They're likely to be regarded as not having enough self-control. And self-control is considered an important quality for executives to have.
Junji: Hey, look at those beautiful little flowers. I never _____ them when I was driving.
Vikram: We miss a lot of things if we move around at car speed.

Listen to the CD and write the questions. Then listen to the conversation again and answer the questions.

1. _____
   _____

2. _____
   _____
3. _____
   _____
4. _____
   _____
5. _____
   _____

READING AND WRITING PRACTICE

A Words and Phrases

architect 建築家   prevention 予防   lose weight 痩せる   love affair 恋愛関係   celebrate ～を祝う   independence 独立／自立   preferable より好ましい   take～into consideration ～を考慮に入れる   residential communities 住宅地   shopping mall 商店街, ショッピングモール   leading to ～につづく   sidewalk 歩道   irrational 不合理な   associate professor 准教授   pollute 汚染する   institute 研究所   survey 調査   resident 住人   gain weight 太る   solution 解決方法   admit 認める   retail 小売りの   issue 問題

B True-False Questions

Read the questions below, and then read the following passage to find the answers.

1. In the U.S. almost half of all adults are considered overweight.   T / F
2. Becoming overweight may have something to do with dependence on cars.   T / F
3. Architects design towns with careful consideration of people's health.   T / F
4. Walking can help people stay in shape and healthy.   T / F
5. If you would like to lose weight, you should walk for at least 30 minutes 5 days a week.   T / F
6. A certain survey says that most people in Atlanta spend more than one and a half hours a day in cars.   T / F
7. A westernized diet may be a big factor in developing obesity.   T / F

Let's Read!

Breaking America's Dependency On Cars

America has a "big" problem—too many people are getting fat. In fact, nearly a third of all adults in the U.S. are considered overweight, according to the Atlanta, Georgia-based Centers for Disease Control and Prevention. One reason for this is that Americans simply don't get enough exercise. It may be because it's not always easy to find a good place to work out. But it also might have to do with America's large size, which means that Americans need their cars—and love them, perhaps too much. America's long-time love affair with the car started when people celebrated the end of World War II. Since then, the car has been a symbol of independence and freedom, preferable to public transportation for most people.

One reason for the country's car dependence is that there just aren't enough places to walk. Experts say better planning of cities is needed, and that architects should take people's health into consideration when they design new offices, parks, residential communities, and shopping malls. Walking is sometimes difficult because of the way cities and communities are designed. Perhaps a family lives on one side of a shopping mall, and yet the roads leading to the stores do not have sidewalks, forcing them to drive. Sometimes fences may also block the way. "We've created an irrational approach to using our land that requires us to use our cars," says Lawrence D. Frank, an associate professor of community and regional planning at the University of British Columbia. "That means there is usually a 'cold start' of the car, which pollutes the air, to go just a short distance."

Walking is an easy way to help people stay in shape and healthy. Some experts say that weight-related diseases, such as heart problems, certain cancers and diabetes, could be cut by nearly a third if people got more exercise. The experts suggest a 30-minute walk, at least five days a week, will help keep the pounds off. Researchers at the Georgia Institute of Technology took a survey on the driving habits of over 10,000 residents of Atlanta, Georgia. They discovered that for every 30 minutes that people spent in cars, they had a 3 percent chance of gaining weight. Most people who took the survey said they spent more than an hour a day in their cars. Public transportation may be the solution to the car problem, says Frank, but, he admits, it's "going to be very difficult for most people to change. We have to start providing retail locations closer to where people live and a connected street network that allows us to walk for non-work purposes."

Can exercise help? Hopefully it will, since being overweight has now become a global issue. But of course, in countries like Japan, where the diet is not entirely westernized, weight increase is not as great as that in the United States, where weight levels are rising faster than anyplace else in the world. (491 words; adapted from "World Affairs 1: Breaking America's Dependency On Cars," *English Zone*, no. 10, July 2004.)

D Summarizing

Read the paragraph again and write appropriate words or phrases in the spaces.

One reason that Americans are becoming obese is that they don't _____. That's because it's hard to find _____, but also because Americans _____ _____. This love affair began _____. For Americans, cars are symbols of _____.

Many Americans have to rely on their cars because there aren't _____. Architects need to consider _____ when they make their designs. Even though people may live close to _____, sometimes roads to the stores don't _____ or fences _____. This is an _____ that often requires _____, which damages the environment by _____.

Walking is _____. Some weight-related diseases could be cut by _____ if people _____. For example, walking _____ could help prevent weight gain. A survey of people in Atlanta, Georgia, found that the more _____, the greater chance they had of _____. Although _____ might be a solution to the car problem, first it will be necessary to _____.

Overweight is now _____, but in _____ it is not so much a problem as in the United States, where _____.

E Speaking/Writing

1. What benefits can we get from cars? What problems are caused by cars? What can we do about them?

2. What would you do if you wanted to lose weight?

Preparation for the TOEIC® TEST

Unit 9

Part 1 — Photographs

34

Look at each picture and listen to four statements. Choose the statement that best describes each picture.

1.

Ⓐ Ⓑ Ⓒ Ⓓ

2.

Ⓐ Ⓑ Ⓒ Ⓓ

Part 2 — Question-Response

35

Listen to a question followed by three responses and then choose the best response.

3. Mark your answer on your answer sheet.   Ⓐ Ⓑ Ⓒ
4. Mark your answer on your answer sheet.   Ⓐ Ⓑ Ⓒ
5. Mark your answer on your answer sheet.   Ⓐ Ⓑ Ⓒ
6. Mark your answer on your answer sheet.   Ⓐ Ⓑ Ⓒ

Part 3 — Short Conversation

36

Listen to a short conversation and answer the three questions below.

7. What is the distributor's problem?   Ⓐ Ⓑ Ⓒ Ⓓ
   (A) They have no stock left.
   (B) Their stock is running low.
   (C) They forgot to order new stock.
   (D) They have not checked their stock.

Unit 9 *Walking for Health: Yours and the Earth's*   59

8. How long will it take for the new stock to reach Australia?   Ⓐ Ⓑ Ⓒ Ⓓ
   (A) Less than a month
   (B) More than a month
   (C) Two weeks
   (D) Two months

9. Who was the woman talking to in the morning?   Ⓐ Ⓑ Ⓒ Ⓓ
   (A) The distributor
   (B) The shipper
   (C) The manufacturer
   (D) The stock clerk

Part 4 — Short Talk

Listen to a short talk and answer the three questions below.

10. What is the special offer?   Ⓐ Ⓑ Ⓒ Ⓓ
    (A) A free can of Coke with any pizza.
    (B) A family pizza for the cost of a can of Coke.
    (C) Fast delivery.
    (D) A family size pizza for $11.95.

11. What is the menu like?   Ⓐ Ⓑ Ⓒ Ⓓ
    (A) There is a limited but delicious range of pizzas and side dishes.
    (B) There are many varieties of pizza.
    (C) It has a hearty atmosphere.
    (D) The menu is suitable for a palace.

12. What is the purpose of the advertisement?   Ⓐ Ⓑ Ⓒ Ⓓ
    (A) To get people to be active and eat pizza.
    (B) To make people smile.
    (C) To promote the restaurant.
    (D) To encourage people to apply for jobs.

Unit 10

Changing Lives

LISTENING PRACTICE

A. Warm-up Activity I: Vocabulary and Phrases

Choose the correct meaning for the following words or phrases from (1) to (14).

( ) refuse to ( ) bully ( ) commit
( ) crime ( ) disturbed ( ) article
( ) juvenile crime ( ) cruel ( ) revise
( ) the Criminal Code ( ) trauma ( ) abuse
( ) patiently ( ) neglect

(1) to treat someone violently or cruelly 虐待する (2) doing something for a long time without becoming annoyed or angry じっくりと (3) a piece of writing about a particular subject in a newspaper or magazine 記事 (4) to change something in order to correct or improve it 改正する (5) to fail to pay attention to or take care of someone 無視する (6) crimes committed by young people who are not yet adults 青少年犯罪 (7) intentionally causing pain or suffering to others. 残忍な (8) mental condition caused by severe shock that may last for a long time 心的外傷 (9) to do something wrong or illegal （罪を）犯す (10) to frighten or hurt a weaker person いじめる (11) laws dealing with crime 刑法 (12) very anxious and unhappy about something 動揺した (13) to say that you will not do something 〜しようとしない (14) activity that involves breaking the law 犯罪

B. Warm-up Activity II

1. Who do you talk with when you have a problem?
2. Why do some children refuse to go to school?
3. What can be done to prevent bullying?

4. Why are more young people committing violent crimes?

5. Do you think Japan is a safe country to live in?

ⓒ Listening Practice

Listen to the conversation and fill in the blanks. Then practice reading with a partner.

Clara: I don't want to watch the news on TV or read newspapers anymore. There's so _____ good news and too much sad news these days.

Rie: Unfortunately, I have to agree with you. I'm especially disturbed when I read articles about _____ juvenile crimes. Some children even commit murder. I don't understand how they can be so cruel.

Clara: Isn't anything being done about it?

Rie: Recently the Juvenile Law was revised because of a _____ of terrible crimes by young teenagers. Now they can be sent to court and punished under the Criminal Code if they are 14 years old or _____.

Clara: I heard about that, but I doubt that revising the law will help reduce the number of _____ juvenile crimes. I think we need to understand *why* young people commit such crimes. Most of them experienced some trauma during _____. Some were bullied by their "friends" at school and some were abused by their parents. They need help.

Rie: Uh-huh. That's why the number of school counselors is _____. One of my friends works as a school counselor. He deals especially with students who refuse to go to school for some reason. He told me that a counselor is not the same as an advisor. Do you know the difference?

Clara: No. What is it?

Rie: Counselors don't give much _____; they just listen to people patiently and try to understand their pain. Many people who are _____ think they have been neglected and denied their humanity. If you show them respect and give them enough time, most of them can _____ a solution by themselves.

Clara: I like that approach. Your friend must be a good counselor.

Listen to the CD and write the questions. Then listen to the conversation again and answer the questions.

1. _____

   _____

2. _____

   _____

3. _____

4. _____

READING AND WRITING PRACTICE

A Words and Phrases

peculiar 特異な, 変わった　　deal with 扱う, 対処する　　qualification 資格　　bar 弁護士業, 法曹界　　revenge 復讐　　bitter つらい, 苦い　　specialize 専門にする　　case 事件, 訴訟　　end up ～ing 最後は～になる　　describe 書き表す　　autobiography 自叙伝　　heartache 心の痛み　　fault あやまち,（過失の）責任　　recall 思い出を語る　　behavior ふるまい　　lose one's way 道に迷う　　blame 責める　　get back at ～に仕返しをする　　motivation 動機　　trivial つまらない　　circuit 巡回　　objective 目標　　organize 整理する　　accomplish 実現する　　humanity 人間性

B True-False Questions

Read the questions below, and then read the following passage to find the answers.

1. Mitsuyo Ohira, a well-known lawyer with a peculiar history, deals especially with juvenile crime.　　T / F
2. Ohira became a lawyer when she was 29 years old.　　T / F
3. Ohira escaped from her terrible situation with her husband's help.　　T / F
4. Ohira passed a lot of qualification tests in addition to the bar exam.　　T / F
5. The desire for revenge prevented Ohira from studying hard.　　T / F
6. Ohira believes that listening to troubled children and trying to understand their bitter feelings is the first important step in helping them.　　T / F

C Let's Read!

From Gangster's Wife to Lawyer

Mitsuyo Ohira, a lawyer in Osaka who specializes in cases dealing with juvenile crime, is well known for her peculiar personal history. She was bullied in the junior high schools she attended, tried to kill herself, joined a teenage gang, and ended up marrying a gangster. She describes these shocking experiences in her best selling autobiography, *Dakara, Anata mo Ikinuite*, which has sold over two million copies in Japan since it was first published in February 2000.

What helped her rise up from the terrible situation she had fallen into was a meeting with an old family friend when she was 22 and working as a bar hostess. "He was the first person to understand my heartache. Before that, not only did people never understand, they said it was all my fault. It was very painful," she recalls.

He was also the first one to speak to her about her behavior, saying, "I know it's not your fault that you lost your way. You were in a bad situation, and your parents and school teachers should be blamed. But you never ever tried to get back on track, and that is your fault!"

Ohira passed several kinds of qualification tests and finally, at age 29, she passed the bar exam. Because she didn't finish junior high school, she had to start by learning kanji. "I thought there was no way to pull myself up other than by getting a license. The desire to get back at those who had bullied me was my motivation for studying," she says. But after passing the exams and being praised and recognized by those around her, she began to think that revenge was trivial.

While working as a lawyer, Ohira has been active on the lecture circuit speaking about her experiences. She can make speeches in English and Korean, having studied them on her own. She still studies English from 4 to 6 a.m. every morning before she goes to work.

Ohira believes image training is important for achieving an objective. When she took the bar exam, she studied hard, imagining herself taking the next exam. She says taking notes helps her organize her thinking in order to accomplish her purpose.

Ohira has met with over 100 troubled children. Her present job is mainly consulting with children who refuse to attend school, many because they are being bullied. When she deals with troubled children who, she says, think they are denied their humanity, she always listens to them, trying to understand their bitter feelings and get close to their hearts, and she tells them, "It's OK to be who you are." It was this way of thinking that helped her get back on track. She does not want children to make the same kind of mistakes she did. "I want to tell them that there are better things in life and that they should not give up hope that things can change." (487 words; adapted from "Mitsuyo Ohira: The Past Is Not for Overcoming, but Accepting," *English Zone*, no. 4, July 2003.)

D Summarizing

Read the paragraph again and write appropriate words or phrases in the spaces.

The well-known lawyer Mitsuyo Ohira specializes in _____, but in her own complicated past she _____, _____, joined a teenage gang, and _____ _____. Her autobiography describing these experiences has sold _____.

She was able to overcome her situation after meeting _____. Before then other people never _____ and said _____.

Her friend said it was not her fault that _____, but it *was* her fault that _____.

Before passing the bar exam, Ohira _____ and started by _____. Her motivation for studying was _____, but she began to think differently after passing _____ and being _____.

Ohira is also active _____ and can make _____.

She thinks that using _____ can help people _____. When she _____, she imagined _____. Another technique that helps her organize _____ is _____.

Ohira's main job now is to consult with _____. She helps them by _____, _____, and _____. She uses this approach because _____ helped her. She wants to encourage children not to _____ and to have _____.

E Speaking/Writing

1. What advice would you give to a child who refused to go to school because of bullying?

2. What can be done to reduce the amount of juvenile crime in Japan?

Preparation for the TOEIC® TEST

Unit 10

Part 1 — Photographs

Look at each picture and listen to four statements. Choose the statement that best describes each picture.

1.

Ⓐ Ⓑ Ⓒ Ⓓ

2.

Ⓐ Ⓑ Ⓒ Ⓓ

Part 2 — Question-Response

Listen to a question followed by three responses and then choose the best response.

3. Mark your answer on your answer sheet.   Ⓐ Ⓑ Ⓒ
4. Mark your answer on your answer sheet.   Ⓐ Ⓑ Ⓒ
5. Mark your answer on your answer sheet.   Ⓐ Ⓑ Ⓒ
6. Mark your answer on your answer sheet.   Ⓐ Ⓑ Ⓒ

Part 3 — Short Conversation

Listen to a short conversation and answer the three questions below.

7. Why is the man surprised?   Ⓐ Ⓑ Ⓒ Ⓓ
    (A) He did not receive any letters.
    (B) He did not receive a package.
    (C) He received a package late.
    (D) His assistant was absent in the morning.

8. Who was the man expecting a package from?
   (A) His company's office in New York
   (B) A courier in New York
   (C) A document company in New York
   (D) A lawyer in New York

9. What does the woman offer to do?
   (A) Search the office for the package
   (B) Call the courier company
   (C) Use her computer to trace the package
   (D) Send an e-mail to the lawyer

Part 4 — Short Talk

Listen to a short talk and answer the three questions below.

10. What has happened?
    (A) Someone has lost a dangerous piece of luggage.
    (B) A strange person has threatened customers and staff.
    (C) A potentially dangerous item has been found in the store.
    (D) A bomb has been found in the store.

11. What are customers and staff instructed not to do?
    (A) Leave immediately by the exits.
    (B) Use the elevators.
    (C) Panic.
    (D) Go to the evacuation area.

12. What made the department store suspicious?
    (A) The item seemed to have no owner.
    (B) The luggage item was left in the store by a strange man.
    (C) The luggage item was not claimed from the lost property department.
    (D) An attendant discovered the item.

Unit 11

How Fast Can We Travel?

LISTENING PRACTICE

A Warm-up Activity I: Vocabulary and Phrases

Choose the correct meaning for the following words or phrases from (1) to (16).

(　) means   (　) favorite   (　) inn
(　) wander around (　) local train   (　) express train
(　) leisurely   (　) scenery   (　) round-trip ticket
(　) do some sightseeing (　) make sense   (　) squeeze into
(　) endure   (　) discomfort   (　) destination
(　) luxurious

(1) a train that stops at most or all stations 普通列車　　(2) expensive and enjoyable 高価で満足感を与える　　(3) the place to which someone is going 目的地　　(4) natural features that are attractive to look at 景色　　(5) feeling of being uncomfortable 不快さ　　(6) to visit interesting buildings and places as a tourist 名所を見て回る　　(7) done without hurrying ゆったりとした　　(8) to experience and deal with something painful or unpleasant 我慢する　　(9) to walk around with no special purpose 歩き回る　　(10) something by which a result is achieved 手段　　(11) to force oneself into a small space 押し込める　　(12) a train that stops only at major stations 急行列車　　(13) small hotel 宿屋　　(14) a ticket that covers travel to a destination and back 往復切符　　(15) liked more than others of the same kind 一番お気に入りの　　(16) to seem reasonable or sensible 道理にかなう

B Warm-up Activity II

1. When you travel, do you like to go by car, train, airplane, or some other means of transportation?

2. Why do you use that kind of transportation?
3. How many days do you usually spend on a trip?
4. Do you have a favorite place that you often visit? Where is it?
5. Where would you like to go if you had enough time and money? Why?

◆C◆ Listening Practice

Listen to the conversation and fill in the blanks. Then practice reading with a partner.

Yuto: Sam, you're back. How was Kanazawa?

Sam: It was wonderful! Kanazawa is a beautiful old town with a long history. I enjoyed staying at a _____ traditional inn and just wandering around the downtown area.

Yuto: You said you were going to go by night _____ to Osaka and then by local train to Kanazawa. It must have taken a long time.

Sam: Yeah, it took almost a _____ day, but I loved that part of the trip. On business trips I take express trains or fly in order to _____ time, but for pleasure I always choose a night ferry and a local train. I can enjoy a leisurely dinner with some beer and then sleep _____ in a bed. And on local trains I can enjoy the beauty of the scenery. If you buy a special round-trip ticket, you can get off at any _____ and do a little sightseeing along the way.

Yuto: That makes a lot of sense. I usually use express trains or airplanes for family trips, but all I can see from them are a series of _____ or a sea of clouds. I squeeze myself into a small seat and just endure the discomfort until we arrive at our destination. But the _____ of a pleasure trip shouldn't be to arrive at a destination quickly; you should enjoy the journey itself.

Sam: It all depends on how much time and money you can spend on your trip and what you want to do. If you have only 2 or 3 days, maybe you should use the _____ means of transportation, but if you have a long vacation and a lot of money, you could go on a luxurious ocean cruise around the world.

Yuto: That _____ me of my childhood dream of taking a dramatic ride on the Orient Express.

Listen to the CD and write the questions. Then listen to the conversation again and answer the questions.

1. _____

2. _____

Unit 11 *How Fast Can We Travel?*   69

3. _____

4. _____

5. _____

READING AND WRITING PRACTICE

A Words and Phrases

drastically 徹底的に, 大胆に　　bidding 入札　　in terms of ～に関して　　enable 可能にする　　reliable 信頼できる　　wheel-on-track レールの上を走る　　disappointment 失望　　billion 10億　　be eager to ～したがる　　edge 強み, 優位性　　manufacturing 製造　　currently 現在　　argument 議論　　maglev リニアモーターカー　　refer to ～のことを言う　　levitate 空中に浮かぶ　　investment 投資　　have second thoughts 考え直す　　undergo 経験する　　afford ～の余裕がある　　due to ～のせいで　　fare 運賃　　candidate 候補

B True-False Questions

Read the questions below, and then read the following passage to find the answers.

1. The Beijing-Shanghai High-Speed Railway would cut traveling time drastically.　T / F
2. TGV technology has already been selected through a fair and open international bidding process.　T / F
3. The Japanese Shinkansen has an advantage in terms of management and operation.　T / F
4. Maglev is a newer technology which enables trains to float above the guide tracks.　T / F
5. Maglev is much safer and more reliable than the traditional wheel-on-track technology.　T / F
6. France's Alstom has already exported its technology to South Korea and Norway.　T / F

C Let's Read!

New Transport System

　The Beijing-Shanghai High-Speed Railway Project has been in the planning stages for more than ten years and has caused many disappointments. The 1,300-kilometer fast link, with a cost calculated at $12 billion, would cut traveling time from 13 hours to less than five hours.

While it was reported that TGV technology by Alstom, a French company, had been selected, China's Ministry of Railways has said that the decision about the technology to be used will be made through a fair and open international bidding process. Formal offers are expected to be made later this year by foreign companies, including Alstom (French), Siemens (German) and Mitsubishi Heavy Industries (Japanese), who are eager to complete the project.

Alstom may have an edge, but Germany's Inter City Express (ICE) technology is stronger in terms of manufacturing, while Japan's high speed trains (Shinkansen) are better in terms of management and operation.

Also, there are currently many arguments over using traditional train tracks and a newer technology known as "maglev." Maglev refers to "magnetic levitation." This is a process which would allow trains, with the help of powerful magnets, to "levitate," or float about one centimeter above guide tracks. Unlike traditional railways, which can only reach speeds of 300-350km/hr, maglev trains will be able to reach speeds of 500km/hr and will not depend on fuel.

China began daily runs of the world's first commercially-operated maglev in Shanghai last year, but the $1.2 billion German-built system is only 30 kilometers long, connecting Shanghai to its four-year-old airport. If maglev technology is used for the entire length of the Beijing-Shanghai high-speed line (1,300km), a total investment of about $52 billion would be required. Traditional wheel-on-track technology, on the other hand, would be only about one-third of the cost

Two recent technical accidents on the Shanghai maglev line have caused more people to have second thoughts about the technology. Cao Yu, an engineering student at Shanghai Tongji University, says, "After all, this technology hasn't undergone the test of time. We just cannot afford the risk on such an important railway line." In addition, due to the huge investment, a high-speed train ticket may be even more expensive than the current air fare.

If it is decided not to use maglev technology, Japan's high-speed technology is a candidate, as the Shinkansen now travels more than 300km/hr. But memories of World War II and the role of the Manchurian railway in Japan's invasion of China during the 1930s have created negative feelings in China about using Japanese technology.

Therefore, France's Alstom may be well-positioned in the competition. It was the first to export its technology, providing Spain and South Korea with high-speed railway systems. In addition, the company set the world record for high-speed wheel-on-track train travel in 1990 at 512km/hr—a record that has yet to be broken.

(474 words; adapted from "On Track or Not?—China's High-Speed Railway Project," *English Zone*, no. 10, July 2004.)

D. Summarizing

Read the paragraph again and write appropriate words or phrases in the spaces.

Although in _____, the Beijing-Shanghai High-Speed Railway Project has _____. When it is finished, trains will travel _____ in _____.

The selection of the technology to be used will _____. Companies from _____, _____, and _____ are hoping to be chosen.

Germany's ICE technology is _____, while Japan's Shinkansen technology is _____.

A decision must also be made about using _____ or _____ Maglev. Maglev technology would allow _____. Trains using it would be able to _____.

China began _____ last year, but the system is _____. If maglev is _____, it would require _____. Traditional technology would require _____.

People are questioning the use of maglev _____. Since the technology has been used only a short time, they can't afford _____.

If _____, Japan would have a good chance, but there are negative feelings in China related to _____ and _____.

As a result, the French company Alstom may have the best chance, because it was _____ and it has _____.

E. Speaking/Writing

1. What means of transportation do you like to use when you travel? Why?

2. Describe your ideal trip.

Preparation for the TOEIC® TEST

Unit 11

Part 1 — Photographs

Look at each picture and listen to four statements. Choose the statement that best describes each picture.

1. Ⓐ Ⓑ Ⓒ Ⓓ

2. Ⓐ Ⓑ Ⓒ Ⓓ

Part 2 — Question-Response

Listen to a question followed by three responses and then choose the best response.

3. Mark your answer on your answer sheet. Ⓐ Ⓑ Ⓒ
4. Mark your answer on your answer sheet. Ⓐ Ⓑ Ⓒ
5. Mark your answer on your answer sheet. Ⓐ Ⓑ Ⓒ
6. Mark your answer on your answer sheet. Ⓐ Ⓑ Ⓒ

Part 3 — Short Conversation

Listen to a short conversation and answer the three questions below.

7. Why was Bob fired?   Ⓐ Ⓑ Ⓒ Ⓓ
   (A) He was not good at his job.
   (B) He made the other staff unhappy.
   (C) He was always late for work.
   (D) He performed badly in his interview.

Unit 11 *How Fast Can We Travel?*

8. What was the problem when Bob was hired?
   (A) He did not have an interview.
   (B) He did not have the correct qualifications.
   (C) He did not show his true character.
   (D) He did not have enough work experience

9. Why is the man a little annoyed with his company?
   (A) It hires too many employees like Bob.
   (B) It pays new employees too much.
   (C) It does not like to fire people.
   (D) It does not test new applicants thoroughly.

Part 4 Short Talk

Listen to a short talk and answer the three questions below.

10. What is happening?
    (A) Some people are giving a cooking class.
    (B) Some people are preparing meals in a restaurant.
    (C) Some people are writing instructions for a recipe.
    (D) Some people are learning how to cook a quiche.

11. What does the teacher advise the people to do?
    (A) Work more quickly.
    (B) Ask more questions.
    (C) Listen to her instructions carefully.
    (D) Divide into two groups.

12. About how long will the dish take to finish?
    (A) 20 minutes.
    (B) 1 hour.
    (C) 1 hour and 20 minutes.
    (D) 120 minutes.

Unit 12

Medical Care for the Whole Person

LISTENING PRACTICE

A Warm-up Activity I: Vocabulary and Phrases

Choose the correct meaning for the following words or phrases from (1) to (12).

( ) treatment   ( ) have a headache   ( ) have a sore throat
( ) have a fever   ( ) temperature   ( ) have no idea
( ) thermometer   ( ) inpatient   ( ) appointment
( ) health insurance card   ( ) sneeze   ( ) drugstore

(1) arrangement to meet or visit someone at a particular time and place 予約
(2) measurement of how hot the body is 体温   (3) a patient who stays in the hospital for one or more nights 入院患者   (4) certificate showing membership in a health insurance program 保険証   (5) instrument for measuring body temperature 体温計
(6) to have air come uncontrollably and noisily through the mouth くしゃみをする
(7) to have pain in the throat のどが痛い   (8) to have a higher than normal body temperature 熱がある   (9) to have pain in the head 頭が痛い   (10) a store that sells medicine 薬局   (11) something that is done to cure an illness or injury 治療
(12) to not know at all 分からない

B Warm-up Activity II

1. How often do you go to see a doctor?
2. Does the doctor give you clear explanations about your illness?
3. How do you feel about the treatment you receive?
4. What do you think about the cost of medical care?
5. Would you like to be a doctor? Why? / Why not?

◆ Listening Practice

Listen to the conversation and fill in the blanks. Then practice reading with a partner.

Keiko: Jane, are you all right? You look _____.

Jane: I *feel* terrible. I have a headache and a very sore throat, and I think I have a fever.

Keiko: You must have _____ _____. What's your temperature?

Jane: I have no idea. I don't have a thermometer.

Keiko: Well, I think you should go to the _____.

Jane: But I'm not sick enough to go to a hospital.

Keiko: I don't mean a *big* hospital. There are many small _____ hospitals in Japan that are similar to a doctor's office in the United States, but there are sometimes rooms for inpatient care. When I have a problem, I always go to Dr. Takaoka's hospital, _____ my apartment. He's very friendly, and he explains everything to me carefully.

Jane: That _____ good, but I'm afraid I won't be able to understand him. I don't know much "medical Japanese" yet.

Keiko: Don't worry. I think he speaks English well, and _____, I'll go with you. Why don't we go right now?

Jane: Don't I need to make an appointment?

Keiko: No. You just go to the hospital, give them your health insurance card, and wait.

Jane: My health insurance card? It's _____ home. We'll have to go there first and… ah- ah- ahhchooo!

Keiko: Bless you. You know, if you're sneezing, you might _____ *me* your cold. I think you should do as the Japanese do, and _____ a mask. Let's stop by a drugstore on the way and buy one.

Listen to the CD and write the questions. Then listen to the conversation again and answer the questions.

1. _____

2. _____

3. _____

4. _____

READING AND WRITING PRACTICE

A Words and Phrases

patient 患者   terminal 末期の   esophageal 食道の   institution 公共施設   free of charge 無料で   recover 回復する   leukemia 白血病   swallow 飲み込む   palliative (苦痛を)一時的に抑える   reduce 減らす   cure 治す   access 利用権   alike 同様に   via ～を使って   frustrated 欲求不満の   lack 欠如   transparency 透明性   exceed ～を超える   appreciate ～のよさを味わう   facility 施設   ward 病棟   confidently 確信を持って   republic 共和国   meltdown 炉心溶融   bone marrow 骨髄   transplant 移植   survive 生き残る   gratitude 感謝   blood poisoning 敗血症   recur 再発する   concern 気遣い

B True-False Questions

Read the questions below, and then read the following passage to find the answers.

1. Dr. Kamata accepted a patient who was in the terminal stage of esophageal cancer.   T / F
2. "Free access" means that everyone can use medical institutions free of charge.   T / F
3. According to Dr. Kamata, many Japanese are satisfied with the present state of medical care.   T / F
4. Most hospitals keep patients until they completely recover from their illness.   T / F
5. Medical care has nothing to do with economics.   T / F
6. Dr. Kamata is president of an organization that supports children suffering from leukemia.   T / F
7. A warm heart is necessary for health care workers.   T / F

C Let's Read!

Minoru Kamata: Providing Empathetic Medical Care

After a large-scale hospital in Tokyo said they couldn't help him anymore, the patient, a 50-year-old taxi driver, went to see Dr. Kamata at Suwa Central Hospital, a public general hospital in Nagano Prefecture. He was in the terminal stages of esophageal cancer and could swallow only water. Though his wife wanted him to receive palliative care (treatment to reduce pain, but not cure an illness), he really wanted to drive a car again. "So we gave him an anti-cancer drug treatment while he stayed in the palliative care unit," says Kamata proudly. "He recovered until he could eat solid food and finally drove himself and his family to Nasu, Tochigi." Is everyone in Japan provided with this type of medical care? Are people satisfied with what they receive? Probably not.

According to Kamata, WHO ranks Japan as having one of the best medical systems in the world. One reason is "free access," which means everyone can choose their medical institutions, and rich and poor alike can receive the same level of medical care via a health insurance system that covers everyone. "Yet," Kamata continues, "I think many Japanese are uncomfortable and frustrated over the present state of medical care." He says the reasons are its lack of transparency and, especially, how coldly some patients have been treated.

In general, hospitals worry about the number of days a patient stays in the hospital; the stay should not exceed the average length in order for it to become profitable. Most hospitals pressure inpatients to leave after a few weeks, after which the patients don't know what to do. "Medical care is connected with economics, but I think its purpose is to help people live," says Kamata.

At Suwa Central Hospital, patients appreciate advanced medical facilities and rehabilitation wards. Patients get 24-hour home medical care as well. As a result, people in Nagano Prefecture have the longest life expectancy while medical costs remain the lowest. "People would accept the medical costs if all hospitals in Japan would do the same things we do here," Kamata says confidently.

Kamata is the president of Japan Chernobyl Foundation (JCF), which mainly supports children of the Republic of Belarus who developed leukemia after the 1986 nuclear meltdown at Chernobyl. With the help of JCF, nine children have received bone marrow transplants; all but one have survived. Kamata visited the dead child's family and was surprised to hear words of gratitude from the mother. She said that when her son had a high fever caused by blood poisoning after transplant, he wanted to eat pineapple. A young Japanese nurse walked around the town in minus 20 degree weather, looking for the hard-to-find fruit, finally returning with some canned pineapple. The boy ate it and recovered, though he died ten months later when leukemia recurred.

Kamata says, "I am confident that, while advanced medical technology can, in fact, cure diseases, a warm heart, the sort of concern the nurse showed the child in Belarus, is also necessary for us health care workers."   (503 words; adapted from "Minoru Kamata: Providing Empathetic Medical Care," *English Zone*, no. 6, November 2003.)

D. Summarizing

Read the paragraph again and write appropriate words or phrases in the spaces.

A 50-year-old taxi driver with _____ could not be helped anymore at _____, so he went to _____. He was so ill he could _____, but he wanted to _____. After receiving _____, he was able to _____ and _____. But most Japanese people are probably not _____ _____.

WHO considers Japan as having _____, in part because there is _____. Dr. Kamata, however, thinks most Japanese are _____ and _____ because of _____ and how _____ are _____.

Usually hospitals worry about _____, which should not _____ _____ to be profitable. Often inpatients are made to _____. Dr. Kamata suggests that the main purpose of medical care is _____, not _____.

Suwa General Hospital provides patients with _____ and _____. Because of this, people in Nagano Prefecture _____. Dr. Kamata is sure that _____ if all hospitals _____.

Dr. Kamata is the president of _____. The main purpose of this group is to _____. The mother of a child who died was thankful because _____ made a great effort to _____ for her son. Unfortunately, he _____.

Dr. Kamata says that although _____, health care workers also need _____.

E. Speaking/Writing

1. Do you have a doctor you usually visit? What is he/she like?

2. What are good and bad points of the current Japanese medical system?

Preparation for the TOEIC® TEST

Unit 12

Part 1 — Photographs

Look at each picture and listen to four statements. Choose the statement that best describes each picture.

1. Ⓐ Ⓑ Ⓒ Ⓓ

2. Ⓐ Ⓑ Ⓒ Ⓓ

Part 2 — Question-Response

Listen to a question followed by three responses and then choose the best response.

3. Mark your answer on your answer sheet. Ⓐ Ⓑ Ⓒ
4. Mark your answer on your answer sheet. Ⓐ Ⓑ Ⓒ
5. Mark your answer on your answer sheet. Ⓐ Ⓑ Ⓒ
6. Mark your answer on your answer sheet. Ⓐ Ⓑ Ⓒ

Part 3 — Short Conversation

Listen to a short conversation and answer the three questions below.

7. How long has it been since the woman smoked a cigarette? Ⓐ Ⓑ Ⓒ Ⓓ
   (A) One day
   (B) Two weeks
   (C) Three months
   (D) One year

8. What is the man's problem?
    (A) He does not want to give up smoking.
    (B) He has tried many times and failed.
    (C) He smokes too many cigarettes each day.
    (D) He wants to stop but does not know how.

9. What advice does the woman give him?
    (A) He should try harder to stop.
    (B) He should cut down on smoking.
    (C) He should stop smoking immediately.
    (D) He should relax and not worry about it.

Part 4 Short Talk

Listen to a short talk and answer the three questions below.

10. What is being advertised?
    (A) A property for sale.
    (B) A package holiday in New York.
    (C) A house for rent in New York.
    (D) Bed and breakfast accommodation.

11. What makes the accommodation ideal?
    (A) People can do their own gardening.
    (B) It has its own tennis courts.
    (C) Its location.
    (D) It is expensive.

12. How long must people rent it for?
    (A) One month.
    (B) One year.
    (C) $7,000 per month.
    (D) As long as they want.

Unit 13

Looking for a Job?

LISTENING PRACTICE

A Warm-up Activity I: Vocabulary and Phrases

Choose the correct meaning for the following words or phrases from (1) to (11).

(　) job interview 　　(　) sophomore 　　(　) quit
(　) feel nervous 　　(　) That depends. 　　(　) Go ahead.
(　) punctual 　　(　) research 　　(　) beforehand
(　) It's a deal. 　　(　) treat

(1) Please begin. さあ始めて.　　(2) second year college or university student 二年生　　(3) before something else happens or is done 前もって　　(4) I agree. Let's do it. そうしよう．話は決まった．　　(5) doing something at the arranged time 時間を守る　　(6) to pay for something for someone おごる　　(7) to feel afraid or anxious about something 緊張する　　(8) to study something carefully and get information about it 調べる　　(9) meeting in which someone is asked questions to see if they are suitable for a job 就職面接　　(10) to leave (school, a job, etc.) やめる　　(11) Maybe or maybe not. それはどうかな？（話の内容次第だ）

B Warm-up Activity II

Answer the following questions.

1. What do you think is the most popular job for women/men?
2. What would you like to be in the future? Why?
3. What kinds of test do you have to take for that job?
4. Do you feel confident about doing well on an interview?
5. Would you prefer to be a freeter?

C. Listening Practice

Listen to the conversation and fill in the blanks. Then practice reading with a partner.

Isabel: You look really good in that _____, Ken. Why are you all dressed up?
Ken: I have a job interview this afternoon.
Isabel: A job interview? But you're _____ a sophomore. Are you going to quit school?
Ken: No, this is for an internship for my future job. It's part of my course _____. Anyway, I feel very nervous.
Isabel: I see. Shall I give you some suggestions for doing well on a job interview?
Ken: I'd appreciate it. How did you _____ them?
Isabel: I was reading a magazine article last night. You're very _____ to see me today.
Ken: That depends. You may make me even more nervous.
Isabel: Don't worry. I _____ you'll thank me after taking my advice.
Ken: All right. Go ahead!
Isabel: First, you should be punctual for the interview. Don't be afraid to smile, act confident, and be friendly to the interviewers. And _____ sure you have researched the company beforehand and are prepared with a few questions so that you can _____ them you're serious about the internship.
Ken: That last point is important. I haven't read the company's pamphlet yet, so I'd better do that right away.
Isabel: And you ought to practice interview questions with someone. Aren't you _____?
Ken: OK. It's a deal! Let's go to the Indian restaurant and I'll treat you to lunch.

Listen to the CD and write the questions. Then listen to the conversation again and answer the questions.

1. _____
2. _____
3. _____
4. _____

Unit 13 *Looking for a Job?*   83

Reading and Writing Practice

A Words and Phrases

characterize 特徴によって分類する   temps 臨時採用者   condition 条件   anxiety 不安   opportunity 機会   except 以外は   self-employed 自営の   ring tones for cell phones 携帯電話の着メロ   security 安定性   make one's living 生活費を稼ぐ   steady job 定職   eventually 最終的には   cut back on 削減する   temporary 一時的な   agency 代理店, 斡旋所   be drawn to ～に興味を引きつけられる   specialty 専門職   diversify 多様化する   register 登録する   social insurance 社会保険   pension 年金   affect 影響を与える   financial standing 財政基盤   average lifetime wage 一生に稼ぐ平均的なお金   assume ～と考える   maintain 維持する   residential tax 住民税   income tax 所得税   performance-based pay system 能力給   outlet チェーン店   employment 雇用   supervisor 監督官

B True-False Questions

Read the questions below, and then read the following passage to find the answers.

1. Sachiko works every day of the year, even on New Year's Day and Obon.   T / F
2. Sachiko is not satisfied with her job because she wants to have her own company.   T / F
3. The government characterizes young girls who wear fashionable clothes as *freeters*.   T / F
4. 70 percent of the *freeters* want to be hired as permanent employees eventually.   T / F
5. The benefits of *seishain* are not much different from temps' conditions.   T / F
6. The growing number of *freeters* may lead to social anxiety.   T / F
7. McDonald's Japan offers middle school students the opportunity to work by having them taste new types of hamburgers.   T / F

C Let's Read!

Staying as a Full-timer or 'Freeter'—But Why?

  Sachiko Miyata works every day of the year, except during the New Year and Obon. The self-employed pianist, opera singer and musician writes music and also makes ring tones for cell phones. Rather than pursuing job security, Miyata is determined to focus on her specialties. "I love my job and I'm happy that I am making my living by doing what I enjoy," says the 25-year-old pianist. "I hope I can play piano as long as I live."

Miyata is one of more than 4.17 million young people characterized by the government as *freeters*—those in the 15-34 age range without steady jobs. A 2003 Cabinet Office White Paper on the national lifestyle found that one in five of all Japanese in that age range are working as *freeters*. While more than 70 percent of the *freeters* wish to eventually be hired as full-time employees, more companies have been cutting back on expenses, letting full-time employees go and hiring temps. Those who are employed through temporary-service agencies are included in the *freeter* category. Like Miyata, some are drawn to specialties, rather than working as general corporate employees.

Employment types are expected to be diversified even more in the future, according to an official from Staff Service Holdings Co., a large temp agency, at which about 1.02 million people were registered as of February this year.

On the other hand, *seishain*, full-time employees, have benefits like bonuses, social insurance and pension plans. While more *freeters* are expected in the future, a report warns that their growing numbers will lead to social anxiety which will badly affect Japan's financial standing. UFJ Institute Ltd. did research in March on the differences of average lifetime wages earned and taxes paid by *freeters* and full-timers, assuming each group maintains the same working style from ages 19 to 60. According to the research, full-timers will earn an average of 3.87 million yen annual salary and a lifetime wage of 215 million yen.

Full-timers pay annual residential taxes of 64,600 yen and income taxes of 134,700 yen. *Freeters*, though, only make 1.06 million yen annually and earn a lifetime wage of 52 million yen, paying only annual residential taxes of 11,800 yen and income taxes of 12,400 yen. According to the report, the number of *freeters* will likely reach 4.76 million by 2010.

Known as a company which puts its part-timers on a performance-based pay system to encourage them, McDonald's Japan invites middle school students to its outlets to offer an opportunity to have some real working experience with supervisors teaching them how to make hamburgers and do other types of jobs, such as cleaning the shop. "We hope the program will serve as a way for children to see the various kinds of jobs available in the world and think about what they want to do in the future," says Sachiko Tawarayama, manager of McDonald's Personnel Department. "Before discussing an employment type, you have to love what you do for a living."

(500 words; adapted from "Staying as a Full-timer or 'Freeter'—But Why?" *English Zone*, no. 9, May 2004.)

◆D◆ Summarizing

Read the paragraph again and write appropriate words or phrases in the spaces.

Sachiko Miyata works every day. She is _____.
Not pursuing job security, she has decided _____. She loves her
job because _____. She hopes
to _____.

Freeters are people _____. A 2003 government report on
the national lifestyle stated that _____. More
and more companies have _____, firing _____ and
hiring _____. Those who are employed through _____ are categorized
as _____.

According to Staff Service Holdings Co. _____.

Seishain, or _____, have benefits like _____, _____ and _____. If the
number of *freeters* increases from now on, there will be more _____ that could
badly _____. According to research by UFJ Institute Ltd., full-
time workers will earn _____ per year and _____
_____.

Full-timers pay annual residential taxes of 64,600 yen and _____.
Freeters make only _____ and earn _____ wage of 52 million yen. They
also pay _____ and _____ of 12,400 yen. According to
_____, there are likely to be _____.

McDonald's Japan, which puts its part-timers _____ to
encourage them, invites middle school students to its outlets to give them _____
_____ with supervisors teaching them how to _____ and
_____. It is hoped that the program will allow children to see various kinds of
jobs and _____.

◆E◆ Speaking/Writing

1. What do you think about freeters?

2. What job would you like to have in the future? Why?

Preparation for the TOEIC® TEST

Unit 13

Part 1 — Photographs

Look at each picture and listen to four statements. Choose the statement that best describes each picture.

1. Ⓐ Ⓑ Ⓒ Ⓓ

2. Ⓐ Ⓑ Ⓒ Ⓓ

Part 2 — Question-Response

Listen to a question followed by three responses and then choose the best response.

3. Mark your answer on your answer sheet.   Ⓐ Ⓑ Ⓒ
4. Mark your answer on your answer sheet.   Ⓐ Ⓑ Ⓒ
5. Mark your answer on your answer sheet.   Ⓐ Ⓑ Ⓒ
6. Mark your answer on your answer sheet.   Ⓐ Ⓑ Ⓒ

Part 3 — Short Conversation

Listen to a short conversation and answer the three questions below.

7. Why does the man not want to give a speech?   Ⓐ Ⓑ Ⓒ Ⓓ
    (A) He does not know Frank very well.
    (B) He does not want to go to the party.
    (C) He is not confident of his ability.
    (D) He thinks Jim is a better speaker than he is.

8. What does the woman want?   (A) (B) (C) (D)
    (A) To have two short speeches
    (B) To have just one long speech
    (C) To make a speech with the man
    (D) To have all Frank's friends say something

9. What is the man's final reaction?   (A) (B) (C) (D)
    (A) He refuses.
    (B) He agrees reluctantly.
    (C) He agrees willingly.
    (D) He says he will think about it.

Part 4 — Short Talk

Listen to a short talk and answer the three questions below.

10. Who is speaking?   (A) (B) (C) (D)
    (A) A parent to their child.
    (B) A manager to an employee.
    (C) A police officer to an offender.
    (D) A school principal to a student.

11. What is going to happen?   (A) (B) (C) (D)
    (A) The person is going to have a criminal record.
    (B) The person must never come back.
    (C) The person will be given a second chance.
    (D) The person will be given a warning.

12. How does the person react?   (A) (B) (C) (D)
    (A) He cries.
    (B) He talks back.
    (C) He willingly accepts the decision.
    (D) He apologizes.

Unit 14

Follow Your Dreams

LISTENING PRACTICE

A. Warm-up Activity I: Vocabulary and Phrases

Choose the correct meaning for the following words or phrases from (1) to (15).

( ) realize one's dream ( ) optimist ( ) pessimist
( ) astronomer ( ) kindergarten ( ) insect
( ) underwater photographer ( ) admire
( ) in common ( ) keen ( ) bare
( ) uneasy ( ) be opposed to ( ) by nature
( ) get along with

(1) according to one's character 生まれつき　　(2) a school for children below elementary school age 幼稚園　　(3) a scientist who studies the sun, moon, stars, etc. 天文学者　　(4) small creature with six legs 昆虫　　(5) person who takes photographs below the surface of the water 水中カメラマン　　(6) to achieve something that you want to do 夢を実現する　　(7) to be against something 〜に反対する　　(8) strong, deep 熱烈　　(9) shared by two or more people 共通した　　(10) person who always expects good things to happen 楽観主義者　　(11) unable to relax or feel comfortable 不安な，落ち着かない　　(12) person who always expects bad things to happen 悲観主義者　　(13) to respect someone for what they are or have done 偉いと思う　　(14) to have a good relationship with 〜とうまくやっていく　　(15) not covered with something 裸の，むきだしの

B. Warm-up Activity II

Answer the following questions.

1. What did you want to be when you were a child?

2. Do you still want to do that, or did something make you change your mind?
3. What do you do when you think you can't realize a dream?
4. Are you an optimist or a pessimist?
5. Do you think people can do anything if they try hard enough?

C Listening Practice

Listen to the conversation and fill in the blanks. Then practice reading with a partner.

Jennifer: I'm doing research on how often people _____ realize their dreams. I know you're studying to become a mathematics teacher, Mari, but was that your dream when you were a child?

Mari: No, I wanted to become an astronomer when I was in kindergarten. I looked at the _____ almost every night. They were so beautiful. After that, I wanted to become an animal trainer, and I was also very interested in _____ insects. But my biggest dream was to become an underwater photographer. I really wanted to do it professionally.

Jennifer: Your dreams all seem to have one thing in common—a keen interest in nature.

Mari: Yes, I can't explain why, but I love nature very much. I feel happy and _____ in nature, but I'm often nervous and uneasy in a crowded city with a lot of tall buildings and almost no bare earth.

Jennifer: So what _____ you decide to become a mathematics teacher?

Mari: My parents were opposed to my becoming an underwater photographer and told me to be more reasonable and _____ about a career. I couldn't fight their objections, so I gave up.

Jennifer: That's really too bad.

Mari: Actually, I'm not unhappy _____ my choice. By nature, I get along well with children, and I think I have a talent for giving good explanations. So I'm studying very hard now.

Jennifer: I really admire your positive _____.

Mari: Well, I try. What was your dream, Jennifer?

Jennifer: Now, don't laugh. My dream was to become a fashion model. I was really _____ about it, but I had to give up because I'm not tall enough.

Mari: Why would I laugh? You're beautiful and slender, and I'm sure you could become a model if you tried. Dreams can come _____, you know.

Listen to the CD and write the questions. Then listen to the conversation again and answer the questions.

1. _____
_____

2. _____
   _____
3. _____
   _____
4. _____
   _____
5. _____
   _____

Reading and Writing Practice

A Words and Phrases

statue ～彫像   gracefully 優雅に   with great precision 実に正確に   transform 姿を変える   Guanyin 観音菩薩   assume 姿勢をとる   breathtaking 息をのむような   coordination 協調, 連携   deaf 耳が聞こえない   China Disabled People's Performing Arts Troupe 中国障害者芸術団   Deng Xiaoping 鄧小平   torture 拷問   troupe 一座   signature piece 代表曲   eve 前夜   Lunar New Year 旧正月   entitle 題名を付ける   Down's syndrome ダウン症   composition 曲   conduct 指揮する   malformed 奇形の   spine 脊椎   erhu 二胡（中国の弦楽器）   amputate 切断する   crutch 松葉杖   property 財産   issue 問題   copyright 著作権   showcase dance 見せ物用の踊り   copy 真似る   choreographer 振付師   appreciation 理解, 評価

B True-False Questions

Read the questions below, and then read the following passage to find the answers.

1. People who are deaf will never be able to dance.   T / F
2. The Disabled People's Arts Troupe includes singers and musicians.   T / F
3. Deng Xiaoping was a famous Chinese dancer.   T / F
4. Since 2002 the troupe has given performances for free.   T / F
5. Watching TV on the eve of the Lunar New Year is popular in China.   T / F
6. The troupe paid a stocking company for advertising.   T / F
7. The troupe has performed abroad, as well as in China.   T / F

Let's Read!

At the center of the stage we see a dancer dressed in gold like a Buddhist statue. As the music begins, she spreads her hands. Then, gracefully but with great precision, more hands appear around and above her. Before our eyes, she is transformed into an image of the Thousand-handed Guanyin. As the dance proceeds, we realize that there are in fact a number of dancers lined up behind the dancer in front, and through their movements Guanyin continues to assume poses of breathtaking beauty.

Such a performance, requiring careful coordination, would be difficult for any dancers, but it is especially challenging for these women because they cannot hear the music. They are deaf and must rely on their feeling of the music's vibration and on signals from assistants standing at the edge of the stage. The dancers are members of the China Disabled People's Performing Arts Troupe, a group made up of dancers, singers, and musicians who each have some physical handicap.

The troupe was founded in 1987 under the guidance of Deng Pufang, son of late Chinese leader Deng Xiaoping. Deng himself is disabled, paralyzed from the waist down as a result of jumping from a third floor window to escape torture during the Cultural Revolution. The troupe began as a non-profit group giving charity performances and spreading the understanding that handicapped people have talent and can be valuable members of society. In 2002, however, it became a commercial group, and its focus has changed from performances by handicapped people to performances by artists who happen to have handicaps.

"Thousand-handed Guanyin" has become the signature piece of the troupe, especially since it was performed in 2005 on the extremely popular variety program shown on television on the eve of the Lunar New Year. There are a number of other acts, however, in the troupe's program entitled "My Dream." One member of the troupe, a young man born with Down's syndrome, memorizes compositions just by hearing them and, with great feeling for the music, conducts an orchestra in performing them. Another young man who has a severely malformed spine plays moving traditional songs on the erhu. One group of dancers, who each have had a leg amputated, use their crutches to form striking designs as they move.

While the troupe's popularity has grown throughout China, some problems have arisen as well. For example, the increasingly well-known image of the Thousand-handed Guanyin has been "borrowed" by a company selling women's stockings and used on the package of its product. More serious intellectual property issues have arisen, with the troupe applying for a copyright on its showcase dance to prevent other dance companies from copying it. At the same time, however, another choreographer has claimed that the dance is her creation and that the copyright would violate her rights.

Nevertheless, the troupe's message of respect for all and appreciation of beauty is spoken in a language that can be understood by people everywhere. Troupe members have visited over 40 foreign countries so far, and if they perform in the ceremonies surrounding the Beijing Olympics, the whole world will be reminded that "Life is full of dreams." (525 words)

Homepage of the China Disabled People's Performing Arts Troupe
http://www.cdppat.org.cn

D Summarizing

Read the paragraph again and write appropriate words or phrases in the spaces.

On stage a number of dancers are _____. The dancer in front is wearing _____. Through the dance she is changed into _____.

The dance is difficult for the women because _____. They are able to do it because they _____ and assistants _____.

The China Disabled People's Performing Arts Troupe was founded by _____ in _____. They gave _____ and _____. In 2002 they began to receive _____ for their performances.

"Thousand-handed Guanyin" is their most _____ piece, but the troupe includes other performers such as _____ and _____.

The troupe has had to deal with some _____ issues related to the _____ of their most famous dance.

The troupe has visited _____ and might be seen by _____ during _____.

E Speaking/Writing

1. Is it important for people to always have a dream they want to realize? Why or why not?

2. Do you think handicapped people have any problems in this country? If so, what are they, and what can be done to solve them?

Preparation for the TOEIC® TEST

Unit 14

Part 1 — Photographs

Look at each picture and listen to four statements. Choose the statement that best describes each picture.

1. Ⓐ Ⓑ Ⓒ Ⓓ

2. Ⓐ Ⓑ Ⓒ Ⓓ

Part 2 — Question-Response

Listen to a question followed by three responses and then choose the best response.

3. Mark your answer on your answer sheet.   Ⓐ Ⓑ Ⓒ
4. Mark your answer on your answer sheet.   Ⓐ Ⓑ Ⓒ
5. Mark your answer on your answer sheet.   Ⓐ Ⓑ Ⓒ
6. Mark your answer on your answer sheet.   Ⓐ Ⓑ Ⓒ

Part 3 — Short Conversation

Listen to a short conversation and answer the three questions below.

7. What is wrong with the man?   Ⓐ Ⓑ Ⓒ Ⓓ
   (A) He has a problem with bleeding.
   (B) He has a problem with breathing.
   (C) He has never been to a hospital before.
   (D) He never goes to a hospital when he is sick.

8. What did the doctor advise him to do? (A)(B)(C)(D)
   (A) To rest for three days
   (B) To take good care of his health
   (C) To have a minor operation
   (D) To do breathing exercises

9. Why is the woman surprised? (A)(B)(C)(D)
   (A) She did not think the man had a problem.
   (B) The man agreed with the doctor's suggestion.
   (C) The man will have to stay in the hospital a long time.
   (D) She thinks the doctor's opinion is wrong.

Part 4 Short Talk

Listen to a short talk and answer the three questions below.

10. What is going to happen? (A)(B)(C)(D)
    (A) People will train to be guides.
    (B) People will tour a campus.
    (C) People will go on a camping tour.
    (D) People will do volunteer work.

11. What kinds of students are at the college? (A)(B)(C)(D)
    (A) Men and women
    (B) Only women
    (C) Only men
    (D) Only foreign students

12. What do students do apart from studying? (A)(B)(C)(D)
    (A) Teach fellow students
    (B) Visit foreign countries
    (C) Take part in voluntary activities
    (D) Support the college strongly

TEXT PRODUCTION STAFF

| edited by | 編集 |
| Kimio Sato | 佐藤 公雄 |

| English-language editing by | 英文校閲 |
| Bill Benfield | ビル・ベンフィールド |

| cover design by | 表紙デザイン |
| ILTS Pty Ltd. | ILTS Pty Ltd. |

CD PRODUCTION STAFF

recorded by	吹き込み者
Melinda Joe (AmE)	メリンダ・ジョー（アメリカ英語）
Lindsay Nelson (AmE)	リンゼー・ネルソン（アメリカ英語）
Edith Kayumi (AmE)	イーディス・カユミ（アメリカ英語）
Howard Colefield (AmE)	ハワード・コールフィールド（アメリカ英語）
Jon Mudryj (AmE)	ジョン・マドレー（アメリカ英語）
Chris Wells (AmE)	クリス・ウェルズ（アメリカ英語）
Steven Ashton (BrE)	スティーブン・アシュトン（イギリス英語）

English Fast Lane
異文化理解のための総合英語

2007年1月20日 初版 発行
2025年3月15日 第7刷 発行

著 者　金森 強
　　　　Jay Ercanbrack　Patricia Lyons
　　　　Annie Marlow　Ron Murphy　折本 素
発行者　佐野 英一郎
発行所　株式会社 成美堂
　　　　〒101-0052　東京都千代田区神田小川町3-22
　　　　TEL 03-3291-2261　FAX 03-3293-5490
　　　　https://www.seibido.co.jp

印刷・製本　（株）方英社

ISBN 978-4-7919-1037-3　　　　　　　　　　　Printed in Japan

・落丁・乱丁本はお取り替えします。
・本書の無断複写は、著作権上の例外を除き著作権侵害となります。

ANSWER SHEET ▶ UNIT 1 Preparation for the TOEIC® TEST

1	Ⓐ Ⓑ Ⓒ Ⓓ	6	Ⓐ Ⓑ Ⓒ	11	Ⓐ Ⓑ Ⓒ Ⓓ	Date	Class	ID No.
2	Ⓐ Ⓑ Ⓒ Ⓓ	7	Ⓐ Ⓑ Ⓒ Ⓓ	12	Ⓐ Ⓑ Ⓒ Ⓓ			
3	Ⓐ Ⓑ Ⓒ	8	Ⓐ Ⓑ Ⓒ Ⓓ			Name		Score
4	Ⓐ Ⓑ Ⓒ	9	Ⓐ Ⓑ Ⓒ Ⓓ					
5	Ⓐ Ⓑ Ⓒ	10	Ⓐ Ⓑ Ⓒ Ⓓ					/12

ANSWER SHEET ▶ UNIT 2 Preparation for the TOEIC® TEST

1	Ⓐ Ⓑ Ⓒ Ⓓ	6	Ⓐ Ⓑ Ⓒ	11	Ⓐ Ⓑ Ⓒ Ⓓ	Date	Class	ID No.
2	Ⓐ Ⓑ Ⓒ Ⓓ	7	Ⓐ Ⓑ Ⓒ Ⓓ	12	Ⓐ Ⓑ Ⓒ Ⓓ			
3	Ⓐ Ⓑ Ⓒ	8	Ⓐ Ⓑ Ⓒ Ⓓ			Name		Score
4	Ⓐ Ⓑ Ⓒ	9	Ⓐ Ⓑ Ⓒ Ⓓ					
5	Ⓐ Ⓑ Ⓒ	10	Ⓐ Ⓑ Ⓒ Ⓓ					/12

ANSWER SHEET ▶ UNIT 3 Preparation for the TOEIC® TEST

1	Ⓐ Ⓑ Ⓒ Ⓓ	6	Ⓐ Ⓑ Ⓒ	11	Ⓐ Ⓑ Ⓒ Ⓓ	Date	Class	ID No.
2	Ⓐ Ⓑ Ⓒ Ⓓ	7	Ⓐ Ⓑ Ⓒ Ⓓ	12	Ⓐ Ⓑ Ⓒ Ⓓ			
3	Ⓐ Ⓑ Ⓒ	8	Ⓐ Ⓑ Ⓒ Ⓓ			Name		Score
4	Ⓐ Ⓑ Ⓒ	9	Ⓐ Ⓑ Ⓒ Ⓓ					
5	Ⓐ Ⓑ Ⓒ	10	Ⓐ Ⓑ Ⓒ Ⓓ					/12

ANSWER SHEET ▶ UNIT 4 Preparation for the TOEIC® TEST

1	Ⓐ Ⓑ Ⓒ Ⓓ	6	Ⓐ Ⓑ Ⓒ	11	Ⓐ Ⓑ Ⓒ Ⓓ	Date	Class	ID No.
2	Ⓐ Ⓑ Ⓒ Ⓓ	7	Ⓐ Ⓑ Ⓒ Ⓓ	12	Ⓐ Ⓑ Ⓒ Ⓓ			
3	Ⓐ Ⓑ Ⓒ	8	Ⓐ Ⓑ Ⓒ Ⓓ			Name		Score
4	Ⓐ Ⓑ Ⓒ	9	Ⓐ Ⓑ Ⓒ Ⓓ					
5	Ⓐ Ⓑ Ⓒ	10	Ⓐ Ⓑ Ⓒ Ⓓ					/12

ANSWER SHEET ▶ UNIT 5 Preparation for the TOEIC® TEST

1	Ⓐ Ⓑ Ⓒ Ⓓ	6	Ⓐ Ⓑ Ⓒ	11	Ⓐ Ⓑ Ⓒ Ⓓ	Date	Class	ID No.
2	Ⓐ Ⓑ Ⓒ Ⓓ	7	Ⓐ Ⓑ Ⓒ Ⓓ	12	Ⓐ Ⓑ Ⓒ Ⓓ			
3	Ⓐ Ⓑ Ⓒ	8	Ⓐ Ⓑ Ⓒ Ⓓ			Name		Score
4	Ⓐ Ⓑ Ⓒ	9	Ⓐ Ⓑ Ⓒ Ⓓ					
5	Ⓐ Ⓑ Ⓒ	10	Ⓐ Ⓑ Ⓒ Ⓓ					/12

ANSWER SHEET ▶ UNIT 6 Preparation for the TOEIC® TEST

1	Ⓐ Ⓑ Ⓒ Ⓓ	6	Ⓐ Ⓑ Ⓒ	11	Ⓐ Ⓑ Ⓒ Ⓓ	Date	Class	ID No.
2	Ⓐ Ⓑ Ⓒ Ⓓ	7	Ⓐ Ⓑ Ⓒ Ⓓ	12	Ⓐ Ⓑ Ⓒ Ⓓ			
3	Ⓐ Ⓑ Ⓒ	8	Ⓐ Ⓑ Ⓒ Ⓓ			Name		Score
4	Ⓐ Ⓑ Ⓒ	9	Ⓐ Ⓑ Ⓒ Ⓓ					
5	Ⓐ Ⓑ Ⓒ	10	Ⓐ Ⓑ Ⓒ Ⓓ					/12

ANSWER SHEET ▶ UNIT 7 Preparation for the TOEIC® TEST

1	Ⓐ Ⓑ Ⓒ Ⓓ	6	Ⓐ Ⓑ Ⓒ	11	Ⓐ Ⓑ Ⓒ Ⓓ	Date	Class	ID No.
2	Ⓐ Ⓑ Ⓒ Ⓓ	7	Ⓐ Ⓑ Ⓒ Ⓓ	12	Ⓐ Ⓑ Ⓒ Ⓓ			
3	Ⓐ Ⓑ Ⓒ	8	Ⓐ Ⓑ Ⓒ Ⓓ			Name		Score
4	Ⓐ Ⓑ Ⓒ	9	Ⓐ Ⓑ Ⓒ Ⓓ					
5	Ⓐ Ⓑ Ⓒ	10	Ⓐ Ⓑ Ⓒ Ⓓ					/12

ANSWER SHEET ▶ UNIT 8　Preparation for the TOEIC® TEST

1	Ⓐ Ⓑ Ⓒ Ⓓ	6	Ⓐ Ⓑ Ⓒ	11	Ⓐ Ⓑ Ⓒ Ⓓ
2	Ⓐ Ⓑ Ⓒ Ⓓ	7	Ⓐ Ⓑ Ⓒ Ⓓ	12	Ⓐ Ⓑ Ⓒ Ⓓ
3	Ⓐ Ⓑ Ⓒ	8	Ⓐ Ⓑ Ⓒ Ⓓ		
4	Ⓐ Ⓑ Ⓒ	9	Ⓐ Ⓑ Ⓒ Ⓓ		
5	Ⓐ Ⓑ Ⓒ	10	Ⓐ Ⓑ Ⓒ Ⓓ		

Date	Class	ID No.
Name		Score　/12

ANSWER SHEET ▶ UNIT 9　Preparation for the TOEIC® TEST

1	Ⓐ Ⓑ Ⓒ Ⓓ	6	Ⓐ Ⓑ Ⓒ	11	Ⓐ Ⓑ Ⓒ Ⓓ
2	Ⓐ Ⓑ Ⓒ Ⓓ	7	Ⓐ Ⓑ Ⓒ Ⓓ	12	Ⓐ Ⓑ Ⓒ Ⓓ
3	Ⓐ Ⓑ Ⓒ	8	Ⓐ Ⓑ Ⓒ Ⓓ		
4	Ⓐ Ⓑ Ⓒ	9	Ⓐ Ⓑ Ⓒ Ⓓ		
5	Ⓐ Ⓑ Ⓒ	10	Ⓐ Ⓑ Ⓒ Ⓓ		

Date	Class	ID No.
Name		Score　/12

ANSWER SHEET ▶ UNIT 10　Preparation for the TOEIC® TEST

1	Ⓐ Ⓑ Ⓒ Ⓓ	6	Ⓐ Ⓑ Ⓒ	11	Ⓐ Ⓑ Ⓒ Ⓓ
2	Ⓐ Ⓑ Ⓒ Ⓓ	7	Ⓐ Ⓑ Ⓒ Ⓓ	12	Ⓐ Ⓑ Ⓒ Ⓓ
3	Ⓐ Ⓑ Ⓒ	8	Ⓐ Ⓑ Ⓒ Ⓓ		
4	Ⓐ Ⓑ Ⓒ	9	Ⓐ Ⓑ Ⓒ Ⓓ		
5	Ⓐ Ⓑ Ⓒ	10	Ⓐ Ⓑ Ⓒ Ⓓ		

Date	Class	ID No.
Name		Score　/12

ANSWER SHEET ▶ UNIT 11　Preparation for the TOEIC® TEST

1	Ⓐ Ⓑ Ⓒ Ⓓ	6	Ⓐ Ⓑ Ⓒ	11	Ⓐ Ⓑ Ⓒ Ⓓ
2	Ⓐ Ⓑ Ⓒ Ⓓ	7	Ⓐ Ⓑ Ⓒ Ⓓ	12	Ⓐ Ⓑ Ⓒ Ⓓ
3	Ⓐ Ⓑ Ⓒ	8	Ⓐ Ⓑ Ⓒ Ⓓ		
4	Ⓐ Ⓑ Ⓒ	9	Ⓐ Ⓑ Ⓒ Ⓓ		
5	Ⓐ Ⓑ Ⓒ	10	Ⓐ Ⓑ Ⓒ Ⓓ		

Date	Class	ID No.
Name		Score　/12

ANSWER SHEET ▶ UNIT 12　Preparation for the TOEIC® TEST

1	Ⓐ Ⓑ Ⓒ Ⓓ	6	Ⓐ Ⓑ Ⓒ	11	Ⓐ Ⓑ Ⓒ Ⓓ
2	Ⓐ Ⓑ Ⓒ Ⓓ	7	Ⓐ Ⓑ Ⓒ Ⓓ	12	Ⓐ Ⓑ Ⓒ Ⓓ
3	Ⓐ Ⓑ Ⓒ	8	Ⓐ Ⓑ Ⓒ Ⓓ		
4	Ⓐ Ⓑ Ⓒ	9	Ⓐ Ⓑ Ⓒ Ⓓ		
5	Ⓐ Ⓑ Ⓒ	10	Ⓐ Ⓑ Ⓒ Ⓓ		

Date	Class	ID No.
Name		Score　/12

ANSWER SHEET ▶ UNIT 13　Preparation for the TOEIC® TEST

1	Ⓐ Ⓑ Ⓒ Ⓓ	6	Ⓐ Ⓑ Ⓒ	11	Ⓐ Ⓑ Ⓒ Ⓓ
2	Ⓐ Ⓑ Ⓒ Ⓓ	7	Ⓐ Ⓑ Ⓒ Ⓓ	12	Ⓐ Ⓑ Ⓒ Ⓓ
3	Ⓐ Ⓑ Ⓒ	8	Ⓐ Ⓑ Ⓒ Ⓓ		
4	Ⓐ Ⓑ Ⓒ	9	Ⓐ Ⓑ Ⓒ Ⓓ		
5	Ⓐ Ⓑ Ⓒ	10	Ⓐ Ⓑ Ⓒ Ⓓ		

Date	Class	ID No.
Name		Score　/12

ANSWER SHEET ▶ UNIT 14　Preparation for the TOEIC® TEST

1	Ⓐ Ⓑ Ⓒ Ⓓ	6	Ⓐ Ⓑ Ⓒ	11	Ⓐ Ⓑ Ⓒ Ⓓ
2	Ⓐ Ⓑ Ⓒ Ⓓ	7	Ⓐ Ⓑ Ⓒ Ⓓ	12	Ⓐ Ⓑ Ⓒ Ⓓ
3	Ⓐ Ⓑ Ⓒ	8	Ⓐ Ⓑ Ⓒ Ⓓ		
4	Ⓐ Ⓑ Ⓒ	9	Ⓐ Ⓑ Ⓒ Ⓓ		
5	Ⓐ Ⓑ Ⓒ	10	Ⓐ Ⓑ Ⓒ Ⓓ		

Date	Class	ID No.
Name		Score　/12